A CUP OF COMFORT®
for
Cat Lovers

Stories that celebrate
our feline friends

Edited by Colleen Sell

Aadamsmedia
Avon, Massachusetts

For Brianna—our little animal whisperer, who loves cats best of all

Published by
Adams Media, an F+W Publications Company
57 Littlefield Street, Avon, MA 02322 U.S.A.
www.adamsmedia.com and *www.cupofcomfort.com*

ISBN-10: 1-59869-654-8
ISBN-13: 978-1-59869-654-7

Printed in the United States of America.

J I H G F E D C B A

Library of Congress Cataloging-in-Publication Data
is available from the publisher.

This publication is designed to provide accurate and authoritative information with regard to the subject matter covered. It is sold with the
understanding that the publisher is not engaged in rendering legal,
accounting, or other professional advice. If legal advice or other expert
assistance is required, the services of a competent professional person
should be sought.
　　　　　　　—From a *Declaration of Principles* jointly adopted by
　　　　　　　　　a Committee of the American Bar Association and
　　　　　　　　　　a Committee of Publishers and Associations

Many of the designations used by manufacturers and sellers to distinguish their products are claimed as trademarks. Where those designations appear in this book and Adams Media was aware of a trademark
claim, the designations have been printed with initial capital letters.

This book is available at quantity discounts for bulk purchases.
For information, please call 1-800-289-0963.

Contents

Acknowledgments

Kudos and thanks to the writers whose stories grace these pages and to the terrific team at Adams Media, especially Meredith O'Hayre, project editor extraordinaire; copyeditor Sandra Smith; Paula Munier, creator of the *Cup of Comfort*® series; and Laura Daly, editorial director.

Introduction

"Cats are connoisseurs of comfort."

~James Herriot

"Cat lovers!" my friend said incredulously, looking at me as if I were nuts. "You're doing a book on cats?" *Yep.* "The whole book?" *Yep.* "Every story?" *Yep.* "How many stories?" *Fifty.* "Fifty! You'll be lucky to get five good stories, much less fifty," he predicted. I just smiled, looking, I suspect, very much like the Cheshire Cat. Smug. Amused. A bit condescending. Certain I'd have no problem finding plenty of uplifting stories about cats and the people who love them.

But even I was surprised at the quantity—as well as the quality—of the stories I received for this book. So much so that I often found myself singing, "There must be 50,000 ways to be a cat lover!" And selecting only fifty, out of more than 3,000 entries, proved to be very difficult.

Reading all those stories gave me a new appreciation for felines and their fanciers. The connection between cats and their chosen people (and it *is* the cat who chooses most of the time) is as rich and complex as a calico's coat, as sweet and tender as a kitten's face, as fierce and true as a cougar with cubs. It has been said that cats are indifferent to humans, and I used to believe that. After reading these stories, I no longer do. I now believe that our cats love us as much as we love them and that the affection and comfort we give to our feline family and friends are returned to us in equal measure. It is a two-way connection, a circle of love.

I've also come to believe that one of the reasons we humans, or at least those who are ailurophiles, are so enamored with cats is that they possess certain characteristics we desire for ourselves but rarely achieve. Who wouldn't want to have these qualities: physical beauty, strength, and agility; an independent spirit; elegance and grace; the ability both to relax completely and to focus completely; the ability to be affectionate and playful at will and for no other reason; expressiveness; courage; discernment; self-possession?

Perhaps that—being self-possessed, comfortable in one's own skin—is the most appealing aspect of the feline personality. Such individuality inspires us to be true to ourselves and to be tolerant of others. That is but one of many life lessons our cats have to teach us—as evidenced by the stories in this book.

One of my favorite quotes about cats is by Eric Gurney:

> *The really great thing about cats is their endless variety. One can pick a cat to fit almost any kind of décor, color, scheme, income, personality, mood. But under the fur, whatever color it may be, there still lies, essentially unchanged, one of the world's free souls.*

The fifty stories featured in *A Cup of Comfort for Cat Lovers* are as varied and engaging as the different cats and cat lovers in the world. Yet each celebrates the quintessential "free soul" of these fascinating creatures and the tremendous comfort they bring to our lives.

—*Colleen Sell*

Silky and the Woman
Whose Hair Smelled Nice

When I was a boy, the cats I knew had jobs, like regular folks. Orange Tom, my father's favorite, and Tom's gray-haired female companion worked in our dairy barn keeping mice out of the feed. They earned a splash of fresh cow's milk twice a day.

It was a beneficial association—legitimate contract labor and one entirely appropriate to a cat's inherent dignity.

Things change. I have a cat now. No barn. Only a cat. My cat, Silky the Siamese, has no idea that mice and feed don't mix. Silky doesn't work for a living, a thing I thought common in the feline world. I have Silky, the unemployed cat, because I wanted my wife.

After I met this really smart, funny, and sweet-smelling woman—after we had snuggled in movie theaters and held hands across restaurant tables and undertaken other semiromantic adventures not requiring feline participation—she began to tell me more about herself, about her childhood, and about a female Siamese cat she'd had for more than twenty years. I learned Tammy—the cat's name, not the woman's—had recently gone to the Great Cat Heaven in the Sky. The woman missed her greatly, and as she told me endearing stories of their two decades together, her eyes welled up with tears.

Nothing will rearrange your opinion of cats like the smell of a woman's hair when she sits on your lap and puts her arms around your neck, which is an activity not requiring feline participation. Of course, the woman wasn't my wife when I first noticed how nice her hair smelled. But I didn't have a cat then, did I?

You and I know from personal experience that men can be shabby creatures, boastful, given to showing off, especially when trying to impress a woman. You know, too, that a man's audition for a lead role in any romantic drama tends toward the frenzied and implausible when a woman sheds tears. You'll not be surprised when I tell you the tears, plus the scent of this woman's hair—*lilacs? roses? lavender?*—had me thinking about finding a barn and kidnapping a cat. I am not ashamed.

I came to my senses the next morning. I knew I'd trip over trouble if I couldn't distinguish the line between love, cats, and gallantry. Instead of committing a feline felony, I began to search eagerly through the want ad sections of every newspaper I could find. Finally, I stumbled onto the one thing that gave me hope that I might be able to waft in the fragrance of that soft brunette hair on a permanent basis:

Siamese kittens. No papers. Excellent pet quality. Two females. One male.

The phone number ending the advertisement belonged to a community a mere seventy miles away.

"Hold me a kitten," I said to the woman who answered the telephone. "A female, please. I need that cat."

Few women can resist a man begging. She promised to keep a kitten until the upcoming weekend.

It was simple to make up an excuse for a Saturday drive with the woman whose hair smelled nice. Early that morning we set out on the Great Cat Adventure. Guess what? The place where the cat lived? It was next to a dynamite factory. An object lesson, an omen, an augury of things to come, I was to learn.

The kitten was beautiful, I must admit. Better yet, it looked just like Tammy, the original. The woman was surprised and suitably impressed. More tears. A hug. I was allowed to sniff her hair for several minutes. I think she even purred, but I couldn't hear her because the kitten was yowling.

As we journeyed home, I discovered a minor flaw in the sequence of happy events I had envisioned unfolding post–cat acquisition. The woman and I were not married then, a celebration my intuition had told me might be delayed until the cat had me housebroken. We set out, kitten on my lap, on the long drive home.

"Ouch! Geez, her little claws are like needles!" I said as we merged from the ramp onto the interstate and the kitten climbed onto my shoulder.

"That's why landlords like mine don't allow people to have cats. Curtains, drapes—those sorts of things can get shredded," said the woman, quite casually.

I looked down at the kitten. I licked the blood from the back of my hand. I realized I had no barn.

The woman began to like me better and to love the cat dearly, but as the days and months passed, I began to think the cat and I simply shared the apartment like housemates who tolerate one another simply to avoid paying half the rent. The only time Silky appeared to enjoy my company was when I decided to have tuna for lunch. She liked the water from the can better than Orange Tom liked fresh cow's milk. The gentle *swhish* when the can opener punctured the top may as well have been a fire alarm. Silky the cat appeared quicker than a volunteer fireman at a 9-1-1 call.

Otherwise, during those early years, I had to be asleep to be within touching distance of the creature. It appeared I had lived my entire life without understanding my feet make a perfect cat bed. If my feet were busy, Silky would agree to sleep on my chest, at least until my incipient asphyxiation. Blood oxygen levels are irrelevant to a Siamese's idea of a good night's rest.

This tale stumbled one step further toward its happily-ever-after ending when the woman whose hair smelled nice became my wife. We bought a house, and the three of us moved in together. Silky adored the woman. The woman adored Silky. I, having had the good sense to marry the woman, sometimes found myself acceptable cat furniture. I accepted those random moments in Silky's company, stroking her fur and speculating on what was transpiring behind her bewitching blue eyes. I knew her presence meant I had been assigned a place in the Siamese universe.

So opens the chapter in Silky's biography where we introduce a new character, Beemer.

I've always liked dogs. I had become the owner
of a house. Houses have yards. No yard is complete
without a dog. I bought a dog. Simple male logic.

It began when the woman whose hair smelled
nice decided she disliked her Volkswagen and wanted
a new car. "A BMW is nice," she offered.

"So are dogs," I agreed.

A successful marriage involves compromise. We
bought the dog instead of the car. I named the dog
Beemer, even though he was neither German nor a
shepherd.

One minor problem. Silky the cat hated Beemer
the dog. Despised, detested, abhorred him—found
him obnoxious to the third power. How do I know
that? Because Silky soiled the carpet. In front of me.
While looking disparagingly at the dog. I shrugged
my shoulders and tried to appear innocent.

The soiling continued, leading me to a funda-
mental discovery relating to cats and discipline. Yelling doesn't work. Neither does a clean litter box.
Neither does escorting them to the door and politely
suggesting alternate sites.

Buying a tile floor does help, though. I only wish
Beemer had told us he didn't like our company and
had moved out before I bought the tile floor.

C'est la vie. At least *avec des chats.*

For years, my primary contact with Silky came only at night, during tuna lunches, and while she sat on my lap to await my wife's attention. That regular intersection of our two not-quite-parallel lives continued until a few days after she ate forty-two inches of thread and then refused to eat anything at all. Veterinarians extract thread from a cat's interior at a cost of precisely $15.42 per inch, in case you're interested. Upon her return home, I mentioned the expense to Silky, holding the bright blue credit card in front of her. She rubbed against it with her nose and hopped into my wife's lap.

Orange Tom, I'm certain, would have offered to get a second job.

For nearly two decades, I, like the graceful bluepoint feline, have tuned myself to respond with affection and appreciation for the love the woman creates and shares. Silky continues to sleep on my feet, acknowledging in her own way that I am part of peace and joy in our home, a refuge that comforts the three of us taking rest on our marriage bed. I try now to never disturb the cat, having learned that the serene rhythm of her breathing resonates from the bottom of the bed and into my heart.

I no longer eat meat, but Silky still craves tuna water, and so the cans are hers alone. Other things have changed as well.

The woman we both adore once insisted on driving seventy miles—in the opposite direction this time, presupposing a belief in Siamese yin and yang—to purchase Dickie, a male kitten of the species. She had the quaint idea that if one Siamese did not revere me, one of the opposite sex might hold a different opinion.

A faulty hypothesis. And another story altogether. One which would begin with my early recognition that Dickie, too, would never be the sort to understand that cats are supposed to work for a living.

It doesn't matter. I still don't have a barn.

—Gary Presley

A Cat in the Bag

Jane stands outside the front door and braces herself. If she completes this mission, then surely anything is possible. "Here goes nothing," she says to herself as she pushes down the door handle. She enters the kitchen, trying not to look too rushed while simultaneously trying not to look too conspicuous.

Her mother is where she always is at this time of day; standing over the kitchen sink, peeling potatoes for an army of three. She doesn't look at Jane. She doesn't need to look to know that one of her daughters has arrived home from school. "You're late, Jane," her mother says without missing a stroke of the peeler.

"Yeah, I got caught up on the way out of school," Jane replies. Not a complete lie, just not the whole truth. Jane didn't want to tell any more lies than necessary; besides, her mother had a built-in lie detector that was on permanent transmission.

"Caught up?" Jane's mum asks.

"Yeah, I got chatting with Pam about this boy she fancies. You know how it is, Mum—girl stuff."

Jane's mother gives a compulsory *"tut"* and raises an eyebrow at the potato in her hand. "Dinner will be ready about five o'clock. Have you got any homework?" her mother asks.

"Loads," Jane answers, bounding up the stairs. Again, not a lie, just not the immediate truth. Jane did have homework, just not school related.

Jane seizes the handle of her bedroom door, makes sure the coast is clear, and then slides into her room and firmly shuts the door. She sighs in relief, but in the next instant wonders whether her mother suspected anything. *Better not to think about it,* Jane tells herself as she moves toward her bed. She carefully puts her hand into her coat pocket and pulls out the illegal load she has just managed to smuggle into the house.

The tiny black kitten sits on Jane's bed, looking groggy and confused. Jane goes over to the wardrobe, not taking her eyes off the precious package, and removes a plastic cat bowl she'd stashed away a few days earlier. She scoops out some tuna from a tin she'd stolen from the kitchen this morning and mashes it into the dish, which she places on the floor. She looks over at her new friend, who is currently sniffing a pillowcase. Mrs. Jameson had said she might not eat straight away and would need time to settle into her new home.

As Jane watched the kitten circling her bed, leaving tiny paw dents in the duvet, she thought about what to call her. "You definitely look like a Sophie," she finally decides, not really knowing why.

"Yes, Sophie it is!" Jane declares, smiling brightly at the kitten.

"The kittens were born at three this morning," Pam told Jane on the way to school several weeks ago. "Mum says you can come over in a few weeks and pick which one you want. I'd go for the small black one; she's a real cutie. I still can't believe you managed to persuade your mum to let you have one. You sure it's still okay?" Pam asked as they turned the corner onto Thornhill Mews.

"Yeah, why wouldn't it be?" Jane replied a little too quickly, knowing full well why it wouldn't be okay and, more to the point, why it isn't okay. She hadn't asked her mother; she already knew what the answer would be. Her mother had no love for pets of any kind, no matter how adorable. The answer would have been no, plain and simple. So she never mentioned the kittens to her mother.

Jane had it all planned out. She would bring home one of the kittens and keep it hidden in her bedroom until it was old enough to go outside. She would let the kitten go outside via the blossom tree conveniently located underneath Jane's bedroom window. The tricky part would be keeping the kitten concealed in her room, but she had already thought that through. Her mother came into her bedroom only when it was a mess, when she needed to put away Jane's clothes, and when she changed the bed linens. As long as Jane kept her room tidy and put away her own laundry and changed her own bedding, there would be no need for her mother to come into her room. The rest of the plan would be easy.

"Wow, Jane! What's that?" Sara, Jane's elder sister, cries as she, quite rudely, enters Jane's room unannounced.

"Quick, shut the door and keep your voice down, will you!" Jane whispers loudly while shutting the door behind Sara, who appears immobilized by the new visitor.

"Is that what I think it is?" Sara asks, knowing full well that it is.

Sara hurries to the bed and begins stroking Sophie's tiny head, besotted in their first meeting. "Jane, Mum is going to have a fit. I take it she doesn't know?"

"And she's not going to, either," Jane says, sitting next to her sister on the bed.

"You can't hide a kitten, Jane," Sara says in a mature manner. "It would be difficult enough hiding it from anyone else's mum, but this is our mum we are talking about, the all-seeing, all-knowing presence."

Sara leaves this thought with Jane for a moment before asking if the kitten has a name.

"Sophie, her name is Sophie," Jane replies with a note of sadness creeping into her voice.

"Dare I ask how Sophie ended up in your bedroom?" Sara inquires.

Jane sighs and tells her sister how she picked up the kitten from Pam's house after school and smuggled her into the house. She tells Sara how she plans to keep Sophie hidden in her bedroom until she is old enough to go outside.

Sara doesn't look convinced.

"You will never get away with it," she says as she tickles Sophie's exposed tummy. "Mum will find her. She will probably smell her before she sees her. What are you going to do about toileting Sophie?"

Jane pulls out a litter tray from underneath her bed. "Ta-dah!" she sings.

"A slight problem . . . there is no litter in it," Sara observes.

"I know. I managed to save up enough money for the tray but not enough for the litter."

"And what are you going to do about food? She can't live off stolen tins of tuna," Sara says, now beginning to sound very much like their mother.

"Oh, but look at her, Sara! Just look at how fluffy and vulnerable she is. Would you have been able to refuse such a tiny, precious angel?" Jane protests.

Gazing into the sweet face and sorrowful eyes of Sophie, Sara takes a deep breath. "No, I probably wouldn't. I am with you on the cuteness thing. I think I would have struggled to bring home just the one. Joking aside, though, you are going to have to tell mum. It wouldn't be fair on Sophie."

"But she'll make me get rid of her. I'll have to take her back to Pam. I don't want to. Sophie is mine." Jane sniffles.

"You never know, Mum might let you keep her," Sara says. Looking first at Sophie and then at her sister, a frown of doubt clouds Sara's face. "On second thought, she probably won't. But think of it this way, if you don't tell Mum and she finds Sophie, she will just take her away without you having a chance to say good-bye."

Jane looks sadly at Sophie, who already appears to have settled in well and is playfully attacking Jane's favorite teddy bear.

"Dinner's ready!" their mother's voice trails up the stairs and under Jane's door. Even Sophie stops what she is doing.

"Coming!" calls Sara. "You are going to have to tell her, Jane. Tell her now before it is too late."

Carefully shutting Jane's door, the girls make their way to the dinning room and take up their usual places at the dinner table. Their mum sets the steaming plates of shepherd's pie in front of them and instructs the girls to dig in.

"Everything all right at school?" she asks, aimed at no specific daughter.

"Everything is fine, Mum," Sara speaks up. "Nothing new to report!"

"What about you, Jane? Anything exciting to tell me? Any school gossip?" she asks.

Jane looks blankly at her mother, then at Sara. Should she tell her now or wait until after their dinner? Her mouth is open, suspended in midair as the silent confession floats out across the dinner table, dancing in front of her mother's eyes, mingling with the steam from the shepherd's pie.

"Ooh, before I forget, I have some good news," their mother says cheerily. "I was in the supermarket last week and bumped into Linda, you know, Pam's mum."

Jane's heart stopped beating, she was sure of it. Ever so slowly, daring not even to blink, she looked over at Sara for reassurance.

"Do you know, she was telling me about that cat of hers, Poncho, the one they thought was a boy and turned out to be a girl," their mother continues. "Well, she had a litter of kittens a few weeks back, and Linda is having a difficult job finding homes for them. Now, I am not keen on household pets, but I couldn't help thinking how you two have never had a pet of your own and, now that you're both a bit older, it might be nice to have something to call your own. It might teach you a bit of responsibility. What do you think, girls?"

Jane didn't know whether to laugh or cry. She couldn't believe her ears. What was she going to do now? She was still going to have to confess, and that would be it—her mum would be so upset they wouldn't be allowed any cat at all. Here was their one chance to have a pet, and now she'd blown it. Why hadn't she asked her mum?

Jane was on the verge of tears as her mother stood up to go get some water for the table.

A large grin elongated her face as she looked down at Jane. "Besides," she says, "you'll need a friend for the one upstairs." Then off she strolled to the kitchen, but not before aiming a well-timed wink at Sara.

—*Maria Dean*

Mountain Mama and the Man of Her Heart

Sierra, a full-grown cougar, had come to us more than two years earlier, when the breeder who'd sold us our first male cub asked if we were open to taking another big cat. These mountain lions were many generations in captivity and hadn't been taken from the wild, but Sierra had been neglected to the point of abuse and removed from her previous home. That's all we needed to know, and we became a two-cat family.

My husband, Allen, built a thirty-two-foot by thirty-two-foot enclosure for our cats, divided into two equal sections by a chain-link wall in the middle. A door in the dividing wall gave us the option of turning them in together. We left large Douglas fir trees growing throughout the space, with the chain-link roof cut out to fit around their trunks. Allen built a couple of platforms several feet off the ground, where the cats could lie in the sun and survey their kingdom. He dug underground dens for privacy as well as for warmth in the winter. Sierra didn't accept Spunky, our half-grown male, so each of the cats had their own den and a large space to run and play.

Sierra's previous home had housed her in a small, gravel-floored kennel, and the pads of her feet were sore and raw from constant pacing. Instead of receiving the raw meat big cats need, she'd been fed dry dog food, and her coat reflected the poor diet.

If Allen approached Sierra's enclosure, she ran to the far side, snarling, hissing, and backing into the corner. She snapped and swatted at him, so he gave her space and time to adjust. He spent dozens of hours outside her natural enclosure, sitting silently or talking softly, before finally stepping inside the door and sinking onto the ground. Weeks passed before Sierra quit crouching in fear or running to the other side of her home, and more time went by before she allowed Allen to touch her.

The vet advised against spaying Sierra, as it could cause a hormonal imbalance. But the cougar-screams she emitted while in heat wore on us, so we decided breeding her might be a better option.

Eventually, Sierra came to trust and accept Allen, but we had no idea how that trust had deepened into love until Sierra gave birth to her first litter of cubs.

That day, I noticed Sierra hadn't been out of her underground den for a couple of hours. Rather than exhibiting the normal pacing she'd been doing the past couple of days, she'd stayed hidden from sight. Because she was an inexperienced mother, we couldn't predict how she'd be with her little ones, so Allen was prepared to intervene, if necessary.

"Allen, you'd better check on Sierra," I called to my husband. "I think she might be having her cubs."

Moments later, the sound of his rapid footsteps coming down the steps emphasized his excitement. Sierra was his own special project. During the fifteen years of our marriage, most of the animals we'd owned were mine or our kids'. That changed with the arrival of our big cats.

"I'll take a look," Allen replied and jogged up the slight rise to her kennel. He unlocked the door and stepped in, carefully closing it behind him. He watched for a few minutes before speaking. "You're right. She's in her den and not coming out."

I stayed outside the chain-link enclosure and kept quiet, because Sierra was a one-man cat and didn't like women. The last thing we wanted was a spooked, upset mountain lion trying to give birth.

Allen lay flat on his stomach and shone his flashlight into the den. "I think she's already had her babies," he called over his shoulder. "I see only one.

I'm going in a little farther. She might be lying on one of them."

His shoulders disappeared, and he remained there for several minutes. Then he slowly backed out.

"There are two cubs. I'm going to stay close but give her some space. They look okay, but I'd feel better waiting awhile."

Allen settled onto the ground near Sierra's den. Fifteen minutes or so passed, then Sierra poked out her head with a newborn, still-damp kitten in her mouth. She glanced at Allen, then headed in the opposite direction and began to pace, apparently unsure what to do with this little bit of fluff. Allen took the opportunity to crawl into the den and check on the other baby.

"It looks smaller than the other one," his voice drifted out to where I sat on a stump outside the enclosure.

"Do you think it's healthy?"

"Yeah, I think so. It just looks a little underdeveloped." He backed out of the den and scooted away from the opening. "I'm going to keep an eye on her. I don't want her hurting one."

Poor Mama didn't know what the little creatures were; worse yet, she had no clue what to do with them. Finally, she deposited the larger cub on the fir needles and headed back underground.

Easing up off the forest floor, Allen walked over quietly and scooped up the baby. He met Sierra at the door of her den as she crawled out with the second cub in her mouth. Holding out the baby, Allen showed it to Sierra, then he crawled partway back into her den and deposited the little one inside. This cycle of behavior continued for some time—with Sierra repeatedly bringing out each of the two babies, carrying them around for several minutes, and dropping them, and then Allen picking them up and returning them to the safety of the den—before Sierra finally calmed down and stayed inside with her cubs.

Allen checked on the new mother throughout the night, and I kept an eye on her the next day, with no repetition of her nervous behavior. But something new transpired on Allen's arrival home. Sierra always reacted when he got out of the car and called her name each afternoon. She'd chirp and answer him repeatedly, until Allen went into her enclosure and scratched behind her ears and she rubbed against his legs in welcome. Often, he'd stay for thirty minutes, visiting with her, sitting on the ground beside her or on a nearby stump or large rock.

A few days after the cubs' birth, when Allen sat on the ground, the big cat trotted back to her den and returned with a kitten in her mouth. I'd brought

our two children up to the enclosure in hope of seeing the babies, but I got a bit nervous when the new
mother seemed to be repeating her bizarre behavior
of a few days before. But instead of pacing, she walked
to where Allen sat and gently laid the tiny, spotted
cub on his lap. Then she went back into the den
and returned with the second baby, depositing that
one, too, on his lap. As the kids and I gazed in silent
astonishment, Sierra sank down on the ground, laid
her head against Allen's leg, and began to purr.

Allen sat entranced, in near disbelief at the
behavior of his big cat. The endless hours he'd
spent sitting on the soft ground of her enclosure
had returned a magnificent reward. A creature rarely
seen in the wild and feared by humans for centuries
had finally grown beyond her fear of people enough
to trust one man and to share her family with the
man who'd won her heart.

—Miralee Ferrell

*The author stresses that cougars are wild animals
and, as such, are unsuitable as family pets. Cougars should be owned and handled only by trained
professionals.*

Calico Bob and the Bamboo Viper

"I thought we were adopting a cat." I froze in shock at the first sight of our tiny new housemate.

"Oh, it's a cat," my wife, Roz, assured me.

"I'll take your word for it."

It did resemble a little white kitten from the nose to about halfway back. The rest looked like a low-budget robotics project. Its hindquarters were shaved bald, and most of them were covered by a series of bandages, splints, and braces all the way down past its back paws. The vet had been merciful enough to leave the fur on the tail. When the robotic kitty creature walked across the floor, its trussed-up hind legs chugged along like a steam locomotive while the splints clacked across the linoleum. The bandaging job was so thorough that we were a long time guessing whether it was a he or a she.

Bob became ours (or did we become Bob's?) after a series of tearful pleas on the part of Roz's friend Carol, who needed to find a new home either for the cat or for herself. Roz and I had recently transferred to my new duty station in the Philippines and obtained married housing, which allowed pets. It was a perfect match for everyone—but me. I was outvoted.

"He will be Bob. Nobody better have a problem with that." I did my best to save some face in the deal. Carol began to protest as she had already been calling it Fluffy or Mittens or some other name no self-respecting cat would choose for itself. But my foot was down. I'd been walked on enough.

Just because a cat lands on its feet doesn't mean it can walk away from the fall. Bob was living proof of that. One day as the kitten was exploring, it climbed too high up a palm tree to figure out a way down. Carol heard mews for help and asked one of the groundskeepers to help get the poor little thing out of the tree. Before Carol could comprehend the cultural differences between the American and Filipino for "get that poor little thing out of the tree," the grounds-keeper assented with a cheerful smile and "No problem, ma'am" and shinnied up the tree, rake in hand.

Carol's cries of "Wait!" went unheard as the groundskeeper approached the kitten, who was poised for battle. She watched in horror as the kitten lost two battles: first with the rake handle, then with gravity. She ran to the kitten where it landed, ignoring the groundskeeper and leaving him baffled that his cheerful efficiency and bravery were not rewarded with some gratuity.

Carol rushed the kitten to the base vet, who worked a miracle or two with pins and chicken wire and lots of kitty anesthesia. The finished product was now interrupting her perusal of her new digs to look me over.

Bob and I did not take too long to get used to one another, and the kitten displayed moments of actual affection after it discovered I was capable of filling the food dish.

Before we knew it, the splints and bandages were off, revealing the even more grotesque-looking bald hindquarters and surgery scars. It was then we learned that Bob was, in fact, a she. (We later learned a bit of kitty genetics: her black and brown calico spots were a dead giveaway to her gender, as all calicos are female.)

With her legs back, Bob was getting around pretty well. The fur on her hindquarters grew back, and she came to resemble a cat rather than a character from an old science fiction B-movie.

Bob did her best to be normal, but her injuries gave her some limitations. She could run, but a bit sideways and always with a limp. We had to be careful how we handled her, lest we aggravate something or other that never quite healed right. What teeth weren't broken grew out at odd angles, giving her somewhat of a hillbilly look. And as much as she purred, she could never manage a meow; the best she could do was a painful squeak.

She avoided heights, except for easy climbs, which included shelves from which she took great care in identifying breakable items and great gusto in knocking them to the floor. She also demonstrated the capability to climb in an emergency, but after a trip up and down a tree, she was pretty much done for the day.

Despite her limitations and quirks, she was still a cat with her hunting instinct intact. We were so mouse-free that we didn't give mice any thought until neighbors complained about theirs. She then turned her attention to the other pests that didn't have the sense to find another house to pester. Her favorites were the geckos that scampered along the walls and ceilings and creeped Roz out. (I kind of liked them.) The word "gecko" would bring Bob charging into the room, where she would transform into a killer with a cold-blooded squeak. That brings to mind one of Bob's more unusual and creepy, even to me, hunting expeditions.

One night Roz picked me up at the airport after a long trip, and on the way home we had an interesting conversation:

"Have you ever heard of bamboo vipers?" she asked.

"Yeah." I did not mention that I'd heard of them at jungle survival school, where they were referred to as "two steppers" because that was as far as you got after they bit you.

"We had one in the house yesterday."

I tried to reply, but my heart had flown into my throat.

She told the story as she drove along. "I came home from the store and heard a commotion. There was Bob in the chair, fighting with this snake. I didn't know what to do, so I called security. By the time they got there, Bob had taken care of the snake. The officer told me what it was."

I was upset at her reaction. Didn't she know that she was supposed to panic at the sight of a deadly reptile in the house?

Roz continued, explaining that the cat looked pretty shaken, so she'd piled Bob into the car and raced to the vet, the security escort doing its best to keep up. There, Bob was pronounced no worse for the wear. The vet figured the cat had gotten some venom on her skin. He said if she'd received an actual bite, she would have been long gone.

"And that stupid snake would be curled up under the chair cushions waiting for us," I speculated out loud. It was not my job to panic, but if nobody else was going to, I had to step up.

By the time I'd arrived home, the snake's entry way had been identified and plugged, and the house was deemed snake-free, so I was able to sleep that night. That didn't stop Bob, though. Over the ensuing months another bamboo viper and a cobra that were foolish enough to wander into her catdom fell victim. So I was still able to sleep at night.

Bob became my hero and a bit of a legend in the neighborhood. She never stopped her playful antics, and neither breakable knickknacks nor geckos were safe. When my tour ended, I was not allowed to bring her to my next duty station. Heartbroken, we sent her to my mother in Montana, where she kept Mom amused, safe, and pest-free for a long time.

The years were good to Bob, but they were numbered. Her time as a hard-living kitten caught up with her faster than any of us would have liked. She loved her short life and made it a point to make us all thankful for every day with her. She is now at the side of Saint Patrick, helping keep heaven serpent-free. All these years later, when life sends a snake through a hole in the doorway, a quiet squeak from above tells me that everything is going to be all right.

—Wayne Hill

Larry: Not Much of a Cat, but Oh, What a Gal!

On Christmas Day, 1988, Larry the cat existed only in the form of a neatly lettered gift certificate from the man of the house, who clearly had run out of ideas. The man of the house famously hated cats, regarding them as unnecessary, at best, and at worst, humorless. He also considered empathy for cats tantamount to betrayal of dogs, and we had one of those.

The gift certificate read: *This card may be redeemed for one cat. I get to name the cat. The cat will be named Larry.*

I knew what Larry would look like—sleek, gray, and handsome. When the spring kitten collection came in at the Humane Society, I hurried over to pick him out. I plucked out dozens of grays and assembled them on the floor, and then added a few random varieties out of a liberal aversion to stereotyping.

One of the random plucks, a nondescript tortoise-shell, was galloping through the scrum, springing straight up and punching the air with a tiny, fuzzy fist. I removed the disruption, stroking it absently, so as to better peruse the assortment of grays. Eventually, I looked back down at my now-quiet handful. The critter was descript, after all: astonishing green eyes and freckled pajamas, belly-side up and limp with joy. I looked at its collar: *Female. PAPRIKA.*

"Come on, Larry," I said to the spotted belly. "Let's go home."

The dog registered no interest at all in the new addition. I sat in the living room and tried out her new name. "Laa-aarry," I sang out in the plaintive nasal tone the name seemed to require. Instantly, the kitten began a careful, circuitous trek from the kitchen, navigating all available furnishings to avoid the floor and keeping the maximum distance from the dog, who remained curled up mid-carpet, the very picture of indifference. Eventually, she reached me and stood on my lap, put one paw on a heartstring, another on the next one up, and then reached up and tapped my nose, twice. From there she ambled with confidence into my heart and began moving furniture around, pulling up the comfy chair. As is often the case, the furniture went in easier than it came out.

After some weeks, Larry's curiosity about the dog had overcome her apprehension. No longer a young dog, she had pulled up at crotchety and was heading toward daft. Ignoring the cat had become her full-time occupation. But for all of that, she still looked rideable. The cat began to stalk her quarry from a high stool, waited, and then launched herself claw-lessly into the air like so much flying fabric. The dog would shrug her off without breaking stride.

One day Larry took a few cautious steps outside, trailing the dog, who wheeled back with uncharac-teristic alertness. Suddenly, Larry had become an outside cat and an item of great and loud interest. Rodeo time! The dog lunged, the cat streaked, and soon both were pinballing madly through the gar-den. This scenario was repeated several times over the next few days, always culminating with one pet in a tree and the other in a victory strut. Any solo excursions Larry attempted were met with a surrepti-tious blast from our water pistol. From Larry's point of view, it was always either rainy or snarly outside. She let it be known, from a soft cushion, that she had intended to be an indoor cat all along.

As a consequence, she never got any of the memos on standard cat behavior. To be sure, early on, answering some primordial urge, she did have a go at the trip-the-human gambit. Unfortunately, she

sidled invisibly in front of the man while he carried
a plate of food, and he promptly pinned her tail with
one foot and launched her belly with the other. It
was sudden, it was noisy, and it concluded with one
man horizontal, one dinner neatly rescued, and a
wildly ricocheting kitten, who traveled forever afterward in our wakes. Any remaining shred of instinct
was trampled out at the same time.

When it came to hunting, for instance, she was
all zeal and no talent. Even moths proved elusive.
Alerted to the presence of a moth by the cat's wildly
swinging head, the man was invariably driven to
counter her ineffectualness by corralling it and lob-
bing it at her, over and over. Once the moth was
damaged beyond airworthiness, Larry was frequently
able to stomp it into lint.

We did encourage her to try for mice, and from
time to time she would collect one, if it were confined, say, to the opened dishwasher and she had a
few minutes to work at it. Eventually she would pluck
it out, transfer it—dangling—to her teeth, parade
for a bit, then put it down and glance around the
room with satisfaction. She never solved the mystery
of the vanishing mouse, which exasperated the man
and further deranged the dog, who certainly knew
what to do with a mouse if she could ever catch one.
At seventeen, Larry scored her first and last mouse

kill. She dropped it on a trap. Dangled trap and mouse from her teeth. Paraded.

But Larry was not without skills. She could hear soft fabric being carefully laid out from anywhere in the house. A quilt top, stretched out just so for precise measurement, accumulated the cat at once. She had a prodigious vocabulary, in more than one language. One of them was the sort in which you roll your *R*s; another was certainly English. We were able to teach her to shake hands for her afternoon snack. She was able to teach us to put away the butter.

She did have a couple of habits, though, that, from a certain narrow perspective—mine—could be considered naughty. She was extremely casual about poop. She ran an efficient, lifelong poop-distribution franchise. Her territory was vast, encompassing any area of the house not otherwise occupied by a litter box. Deliveries arrived daily, in no discernable pattern, the work of a rogue Easter bunny. She was never a malicious animal, and in this, too, she had no malice aforethought; in fact, no forethought whatsoever. The decision to poop and the deposition of poop were nearly simultaneous events. And if this resulted in a random turd rolling up against her food dish or in her cat bed, well, she was not one to lose sleep over it . . . or, for that matter, right on it.

She also loved our furniture—loved it to ribbons. But in the absence of anything upholstered, she had no idea what to do with her claws, so they remained tucked away. As a result, petting the cat grew to be a fairly energetic event. During one of these sessions, with the cat flattened, upside-down, fur rumpled into quills, I mused about her name, which had come to seem exactly right. What in the world would we name our next cat?

"I think we might as well call it 'Slash,'" the man said.

This was a man of big heart and boundless love, which he was happiest inflicting on anyone who could take a good teasing. Any untroubled and unarmed soul was likely prey. He observed the cat and began to ponder the possibilities. Pat-a-cake was introduced to the unwary animal, stretched out against a long lap. Cakes were rolled, pricked, and marked with a B. Larry was not, truth be told, much enamored of throwing it in the oven for Baby and Me, but she had no idea how a cat could get out of such a gig; and it clearly meant a lot to the big, warm man. So cakes were thrown.

In fact, neither the man nor his new little buddy were very well informed about cat protocol, which became clear to me when I overheard him singing, "Rooo-oooll over!" in an encouraging falsetto.

I rolled my eyes. He was bent over the cat, demonstrating the concept with little spinning motions of his arms. Undaunted, he continued his tutorial, until the day his request was followed with a heartfelt "Good kitty!" I ran into the room, a scene of elation. The man had the cat rumpled flat, squeezing out a mighty purr. She traded a rollover for a good rumpling ever after.

After a time, one might happen to observe, if one approached with enough stealth, the man petting the cat in his lap.

"I thought you hated cats." I smirked.

"I do," he replied. "They hate this." Petting resumed. "Really not much of a cat," he added under his breath, with a note of approval.

How far could a relationship go between an unusually good-natured cat and an alarmingly affectionate man? The two seemed destined to find out, one always pushing the envelope and the other content to bat the pencil off the table. What were the limits of feline forbearance? One would have guessed—but one would have been wrong—that they might have been reached at the invention of Kitty Bowling. Kitty Bowling required an expanse of slick flooring and a trio of empty plastic soda bottles. The ball was rolled up and poured out into the lane, with a precise minimum of gusto, and though she generally righted herself in time to vault the pins, occasionally she ticked one with her foot. The man was the first to admit that the ball return tended to be pretty slow. He never did pick up a spare. But the ball did return.

The dog, meanwhile, had long since slid into senility and out of the picture, and after a cautious ten years or so, Larry began to venture out onto the back porch to have a cigarette with the man. They smoked companionably enough for a few seasons until they were able to quit; after, Larry was no longer discouraged from coming outside to the patio to sit a spell. A slight warning tone from the humans soon demonstrated the allowable limits. With nothing keeping her from straying off the patio but the expectation that she wouldn't, her paws would remain poised precisely at the edge, head fully turtled out to nibble at a blade of grass. When we called, she trotted back inside. Neighbors seemed incredulous. But then, they also took the hand-shaking routine to be very clever, not realizing how long it had taken to break her of shaking with her left hand.

All went well for over seventeen years, with Larry and me sharing the burden of a man's boisterous love, until the day she appeared to lose interest in her food. She still bounded into her snack chair and shook hands, but the treat remained untouched.

Decline was rapid. After a few days, we took her in to the doctor, who had nothing good to say. An array of punishments—pills, needles—was offered to keep her "comfortable" for another few months. We went home.

Two days later she was two days worse. I was not interested in seeing what the fourth day would bring. As it turned out, I loved her enough to make a deal with the devil, with whom I already had a working relationship, but too much to make the deal with the veterinarian. We brought her in one last time.

All the next day the furniture in my heart was on the move again, crashing about. The man of the house was faring no better. "Damn cat," he gasped, honking. "I hate cats."

It's a cat's last clever trick. The most unlikely things yank out a sob—an unmolested quilt top; a single, tiny, final turd left precisely in the center of the litter box. We try to coax her into the past tense, but still she remains just in the next room, about to stroll in. Sometimes, apparently, the past tense resides in the future. Slash has yet to be conceived.

—*Murr Brewster*

Fraidy Cat

The boy found the cat tucked far under the front porch. We lived a few feet from a busy street, so making it from wherever he'd come from to our porch was testament enough to his determination. And the connection we saw form in the weeks and months to come was a true testament of friendship between a cat and a boy.

The boy came to us just weeks before the kitten was found mewing and terrified below the porch. The boy had come in much the same way. Eight years old, he was brought to my home late one evening in a police cruiser after having been removed from his tenth foster home. He, too, was scared yet determined.

"I don't let nobody under my covers no more," he announced upon arrival.

"That's a good idea," I told him.

He slept in a cushy armchair that first night and for many nights to come. He was afraid of beds, afraid of windows, afraid of almost everything.

On his third day in our home, the blue eyes that knew too much looked up at me and asked, "Can I live here a long time, like three months?"

"Well, that's not very long," I said.

He thought for a moment. "Well, how 'bout till I'm thirteen?"

That's when I knew this boy had no concept of family, of forever. I called his caseworker to see what the plan was for permanency, and there wasn't one. "We'll keep him," I said, and they didn't argue, because nobody else wanted him. Much like the cat.

When the boy found the cat terrified in the dark corner, something clicked between them. Not right away, as neither one had reason to trust, and they didn't. Both had reason to hate, and they did.

It took three days for the boy to coax the kitten out into daylight. It took two more to lead him into the garage, where he could then be guided into the house after several more days of coaxing. The boy was determined to save that cat. Perhaps he wished someone had tried harder to save him when he was so little and afraid. Perhaps he saw himself in the tremors and cries that each movement evoked from the tiny creature.

By the time the cat entered the house and hid behind the couch, the boy had named him Fraidy Cat. He set food out on the floor at the edge of the couch where the dark met the light, and he stood back to wait. Nothing. He lay down on his belly and watched the dark crevice against the wall. Patient as any kid has ever been, the boy—despite attention deficit disorder, fetal alcohol syndrome, and being born addicted to methamphetamines—waited for that cat to come out. For hours, for days, he waited. While the boy slept in the chair, the kitten watched. Sometimes while the boy slept the food disappeared, and he was happy knowing the kitten was eating.

One day the little guy stuck a nose out from behind the couch. The boy was there, watching, patient and curious. Fraidy marched right up to the boy, sniffed, mewed, and sat, looking eye-to-eye at his new owner. The boy had not chosen the cat; the cat had chosen the boy. Nobody had ever done that before—wanted him.

That night, Fraidy and the boy slept in a bed. First something had to be done about the window next to the bed. Though it was covered with a curtain, the gaps at the edges terrified the boy, so we duct-taped them to the wall.

In the weeks and months to come, fear became more and more a part of their past. Fraidy still would not come to anybody else, but he let the boy carry him everywhere. They played games, swung on the swing set, jumped on the trampoline. The boy lugged him up and down the stairs and all around the house, and each night he carried him to bed, where they snuggled down under the covers, where nobody goes anymore, and slept safely and soundly. Their journey of trust had begun.

Three years have passed since that summer night when the boy and the kitten came together in my home. Last night I scurried around getting kids off to bed, the five we have now going off in different directions. The boy came into the living room, where Fraidy, now huge and sleek, lounged lazily on the back of the couch he had once hidden behind. The boy no longer carries him, he just calls his name. "Come on, Fraidy, it's time for bed."

The cat rose slowly from his spot, stretched his back tall in his I'll-come-in-my-own-time way, and hopped down after the boy. He followed closely on the boy's heels as they plodded off to bed.

I wandered in to turn off the bedroom lights and found Fraidy and the boy snuggled into the big bed, where they sleep together each night. There is no fear in this room, where the curtains flutter in the breeze of the open window.

—*Keri Ann Collins*

Phantom of the Apartment

"I can't take him with me," she said. "I can't get him out of the closet."

"He's a cat, not a wild mountain lion."

"You try it."

The closet wasn't very big, just a garden-variety recess in the wall with sliding doors that had a tendency to fall off the track and onto your head. I turned on the hall light to see into the back of the closet. Just as I caught sight of the furry shadow with glowing amber eyes in the far corner, the light went out. I jumped and screamed. Reflex.

"I told you so," Marla said.

"Does that always happen?" I reached into a box and pulled out a lightbulb. "Wow! This box is full of lightbulbs."

I centered the step stool Marla brought me under the ceiling light, climbed up, and replaced the bulb, dropping the burned-out bulb into Marla's hands.

"Every single time." She sighed. "It's not scary really, just strange, and it's only this light." She slid the closet door shut. "Mr. Hyde came with the apartment, and now he's yours."

"I wanted a pet, but I was thinking a kitten."

"You could still have a kitten, but Mr. Hyde stays."

I glanced back at the closet. "Does he ever come out of there? How do you feed him?"

"Put the food out. He'll eat." Marla picked up the box of lightbulbs and headed for the door. "He prefers Tender Vittles." As if unable to make up her mind, Marla hesitated at the door, looked down at the box, and set it back down. "You'll need these," she said, and left—leaving me with a cat. A black cat.

I shook my head and smiled. Maybe he'd be like Shadow, who used to lie in front of the keyboard while I worked and sleep on the pillow next to me, when he wasn't stretched out across my neck, apparently unaware he was no longer a kitten and weighed half a ton.

After unpacking the dishes and putting them away, I checked the refrigerator. Empty. I needed food; so did Mr. Hyde. Right, Tender Vittles. Maybe they were on sale.

Over the next few days the food disappeared, but Mr. Hyde made not a single appearance. Three bulbs burned out before I stopped looking at the corner where the shadows were darkest and two large yellow orbs blinked up at me. Clearly, he wasn't starving, but I began to long for the feel of soft fur and the sound of contented purring. But Mr. Hyde evidently wasn't the kind of cat that slept on desks or pillows. I gave up trying to coax him out and enjoyed my new apartment with the fireplace in the bedroom.

A week later, Mr. Hyde came out of the closet.

I had just stretched the kinks out of my back and was settling in for two more hours of work. Just as I put on the headphones and settled my fingers on the keyboard, I jumped straight up out of my chair—with Mr. Hyde's claws firmly anchored to my backside. He dropped off and landed softly on the floor as I looked at the blood on my fingertips. He stared up at me, golden eyes all innocence, and meowed. He was coal black, without a single white hair anywhere, with eyes a rich, clear amber. He was beautiful. As I bent down to pet him, Mr. Hyde meowed again, got up, walked to the door, and stopped to look over his shoulder. He wanted me to follow him.

I did.

Right into the kitchen.

His water bowl was empty, and only two pieces of kibble were left in his bowl. He sat down and waited, silently and patiently looking up at me. I obliged and filled his dishes. Mr. Hyde put out a paw and tipped over the bowl. He looked up at me. I filled the bowl, and he tipped it over again. I mopped up the water. Before I put down another bowl of water for him to spill, on a hunch I washed out the bowl, filled it, and set it back down. Mr. Hyde drank delicately and then tucked into his food. I was dismissed.

Over the next few weeks, between sudden attacks of lancing claws in my backside and Mr. Hyde's yowls when I forgot he was lying behind my chair and slid back, catching his tail fur in the wheels, which was beginning to look quite bald in places, we settled into a comfortable working relationship. He even ventured to sleep at the foot of the bed on the unoccupied side, but wouldn't move any closer.

For a year we rubbed along very comfortably, or at least he did, since I couldn't figure out how to sink my claws into his tender hide. But then he couldn't roll his chair over my tail fur and leave me bald, either. Our relationship worked, except when I had guests. A knock on the door sent Mr. Hyde skidding across the tile floor into the closet, passing through the closed doors as if by magic.

My friends thought I had lost my mind, leaving out food and water for a phantom cat. I could never coax Mr. Hyde out of the closet, and the bulbs kept blowing out when I opened the closet door to prove he was down in the corner behind a box of Christmas decorations. I suppose it was no weirder than some of my friends' pets, or relationships. Then the time came for me to move again.

"You'll love Dallas," my boyfriend said over the phone, "and I know you love me."

"I don't want to move to Texas," I said, glancing out the window at the trees and the little green shoots showing between patches of melting snow. I'd planted crocuses and tulips the fall before, and soon the roses would be in full bloom. "It doesn't snow down there, and it's hot and dusty."

"We get snow—occasionally." He sighed. "Don't you want to marry me?"

I did, but . . . "Yes."

"All right then. How soon can you get here?"

"A month."

"That's too long. I miss you."

"A month. I need to make arrangements, get some things into storage, pack, and . . ." I looked around. There wouldn't be a fireplace in the bedroom in Dallas. "A month."

How would I get Mr. Hyde out of the closet? I didn't want to leave him behind.

I handed the keys to Phillip. "Well, that's it. You know how to work the propane heater, and the plumber will be by to fix the sink tomorrow. The truck should be here at about four o'clock to pick up the bookcases." I picked up the box of lightbulbs and handed them to Phillip. "You'll need these, too."

"Why would I need that many lightbulbs?"

"For the hall light near the closet."

Phillip chuckled. "Oh, the phantom cat."

"He likes Tender Vittles, and make sure to wash his bowls every time you feed him."

"No one has seen your cat."

"And yet the food keeps disappearing." I took his arm and led him to the closet, carrying the step stool with me. Opening the step stool and centering it under the ceiling light, I held out a bulb. "Go on. Open the door and look inside."

Phillip reached for the door.

"Be careful, or it will . . ."

The door fell on his head.

"It does that sometimes."

Phillip rubbed his forehead. "Thanks for telling me. Anything else I should know?" He propped the door up against the wall.

"You'll see."

"Will it hurt?"

I gestured to the closet. "See for yourself."

Phillip opened the door and looked where I pointed.

"Hey," he said, "there's something in there." He'd spotted the glowing amber eyes in the darkest shadow in the corner. "It's a cat."

The hall light went out.

"That's Mr. Hyde. He goes with the apartment."

"I don't want a cat."

Placing the lightbulb in his hand and urging him to climb the stool, I nodded. "He'll get used to you." He handed me the burned-out bulb, and I tossed it into the trash on my way out the door.

"One more thing, Phillip. Never sit with your back exposed."

"Why?"

"You'll figure it out."

—*J. M. Cornwell*

Man's Best Friend

Knitting relaxes me. As my fingers work the needles and the yarn unwinds, something beautiful emerges. I'm content—and so is my nine-year-old black-and-white tuxedo cat, who loves to curl up on the soft wool of my latest project and purr. Although Ben is technically my pet, my husband and I share parental responsibility for Ben and love him dearly. But, in truth, he's really a "daddy's boy."

Since our kids are all grown and live away from home, Ben has been raised like an only child. He's received more attention than many people give their human children. As far as he's concerned, I've been a stay-at-home mom purely for his benefit, not because I run a home-based business. And his dismay over his "dad" holding jobs out in the real world has been clear.

Acutely attuned to our daily schedules, particularly Jorgie's, each morning before the alarm clock could sound, Ben would jump in the bed beside his dad and snuggle with him, demanding to be rubbed and scratched behind the ear. If the alarm didn't go off or if Ben didn't get the attention he thought he deserved, his dad's handlebar mustache would get tugged or his face would receive several licks with Ben's rough tongue.

To say these two had a definite morning routine is a massive understatement. From the time they got up and ready for their day, through breakfast, and until Jorgie left for work, they would talk to each other and play, with Ben following every footstep Jorgie took. Then Ben would make his way back to the bedroom, announce his presence with an *auk* and proceed to take over Jorgie's spot in the bed with a huge sigh.

Later, when I got up, Ben would get a second breakfast, one that I knew from his expression wasn't as good as what he'd received earlier. After managing to eat his unappetizing meal, Ben would settle into his routine with me, mostly helping me type and napping, and bide his time until his playmate returned from work.

Back then, Jorgie worked a lot of overtime, so it was difficult for me to know when he'd arrive home. Somehow, Ben knew. While I continued to work or fix supper, Ben would park himself in our living room bay window and watch for Jorgie's red truck to come down the street. And he always knew before I did when it turned into the driveway. Ben's nails would clatter on the wooden stairs as he raced for the den door to greet Jorgie and twine himself around his legs. All was well again in Ben's world. His dad was home.

If it seems like our life was simplistic and routine, maybe it was. Jorgie and I always joked that we were just two boring people, and Ben fit right into our little family. Excitement and drama were for other people. As far as we were concerned, life was good. Comfortable. Happy.

The morning of May 5, 2006, changed all of that. And it changed each of us.

I awoke earlier than usual. Something wasn't right. Jorgie's side of the bed was empty, and Ben wasn't in his place. I listened for those familiar morning routine sounds from downstairs, but the house was oddly silent. Then I heard Jorgie's footsteps on the stairs. There was an unusual heaviness to them as he made his way to our bedroom. Then it hit me. There was only the single set of footsteps. Alarmed, I sat up in bed and glanced at the clock. It was after 8:00 A.M. Jorgie usually left for work a little after 7:00. Finally, I heard Ben's nails on the floor. Soft. Hesitant. Pacing. He never paced.

My heartbeat accelerated as I tried to find my voice. I'm usually not an alarmist, but my mind raced through a dozen scenarios, each worse than the one before. *Was there something wrong with my elderly father? Had someone in the family had an accident? Was someone dead?*

I couldn't summon my voice. And Ben continued to pace between his dad's side of the bed and the doorway to the hall.

At last, Jorgie spoke, in a tone I hadn't heard from him before, small and scared. "I think you need to take me to the emergency room. I'm bleeding."

Suddenly, time, which had seemed to go in slow motion just moments before, was now moving at warp speed. I still don't remember getting dressed and driving to the hospital. And as we raced out the door, I was only vaguely aware of the look on Ben's face: worried. That's the only way to describe it. He was scared. And so was I.

Endless hours later, we knew nothing other than something was seriously wrong with Jorgie. The doctors wanted to admit him, but it was Friday, the beginning of the weekend, and we knew not a lot would happen diagnostically until Monday. Besides, Jorgie wanted to go home. Reluctantly, the doctors agreed. After a specialist appointment was scheduled for the start of the work week and Jorgie was fitted with some equipment and instructions, we were allowed to leave.

When we arrived home, an anxious Ben greeted us and then immediately shied away. The strong smells of the hospital lingered on our clothes and bodies, and our darling wanted none of it.

That weekend we tried to act as normal as possible, despite the abnormal circumstances, the equipment hooked up to Jorgie, and the pervasive fear that hung over us like a thundercloud. Poor Ben was confused and neglected in comparison to usual. No longer was he the center of our world; Jorgie's medical condition had become the focus of our energy and attention.

That didn't change over the following few weeks. Weeks that brought a slew of doctors' appointments, endless tests, surgery, and finally a diagnosis.

Cancer.

The word we dreaded. The word we feared.

The specialist told us that Jorgie would need extensive surgery, if his body could withstand it. More tests. More specialists. As each one signed off on the surgery, we had hope. Without the surgery, Jorgie would die. With the surgery, he had a chance. We held on for that.

To say our daily routine changed drastically is an understatement. Our lives changed even more. And our beloved Ben took a backseat to the disease that was ruling our lives.

As his dad grew weaker, Ben sank into a depression. No longer did he rush to meet his dad when we'd return from yet another medical appointment.

He dragged to the door with a heaviness that almost broke my heart. Somehow he knew what the stakes were. Somehow he knew what we were up against.

One night after a particularly rough day, my husband and I lay in bed, both too tired to sleep, just trying to relax. Ben had been missing in action for a while, but that wasn't unusual these days. He couldn't stand those antiseptic smells that seemed to surround us. Normally, I'd go look for Ben, but not tonight. Tonight I was beat. Ben would have to fend for himself.

Then I heard the familiar click, click, clicking of his sharp nails striking the wooden floor. But his steps were hesitant, like he was struggling with a particularly heavy load. The footsteps stopped by his dad's side of the bed for the first time in weeks. Then he let out a sound that can only be described as a keening, a raw animalistic sound of pain and loss.

Stunned, Jorgie and I both sat up in bed. Beside Ben, who was still stationed at his dad's bedside, was a mammoth white ball of yarn. Yarn that was almost as big as he was. Yarn that I thought had been safely stored away in a guest room closet.

Then Ben cried out again. The sound ripped through me. I got up to check him for injuries and was relieved to see that he was fine, at least physically. As I rubbed him on his back, he purred, a sound that we suddenly realized had been missing for weeks. Jorgie and I praised Ben for his gift. And he purred some more.

Mindful of the tubing and equipment hooked up to Jorgie, Ben climbed into bed and slept with us that night. It was as if he had finally found a way to express himself, to tell us how he felt about his dad's illness and the impact it was having on our family.

After several long weeks, Jorgie's major surgery was finally scheduled for June 19. Ben continued to haul balls of yarn up and down the two flights of stairs that separate our den from our bedroom. Each time he deposited a ball of yarn at his dad's feet, he'd let out that keening sound. And then purr.

Yarn was everywhere—balls and skeins of all colors, shapes, and sizes. If Ben could find it, he found a way to carry it. Once he had exhausted his stash of yarn, Ben moved on to fuzzy knitted winter scarves. He carried these in his teeth and dragged them between his legs, fighting the stairs and household objects, to bring Jorgie something to cheer him up and to express his love for his dad.

And our spirits did lift with each gift this valiant cat brought. It was as if he were telling his dad that everything was going to be okay. Both Jorgie and I felt Ben's deep caring and concern, his unconditional love. Who says cats are independent and standoffish? Well, they haven't met our darling boy.

Jorgie's surgery lasted more than ten hours. A week later he came home minus a few body parts and with a lengthy recovery ahead of him. And Ben was there to greet him . . . with a ball of yarn.

More surgeries followed. More hospital smells. More equipment. But Ben didn't shy away, not since he'd figured out what he needed to do.

Our lives had evolved into a new normal. Jorgie's cancer changed us. It had made us more aware of the fragility and preciousness of time together. It made us appreciate the simple joy of a ball of yarn given by one who gives with all of his heart and soul.

Jorgie retired and is home all of the time now. He and Ben have developed a new daily routine. They both rest more than before and take their catnaps in the afternoon.

Ben has stopped carrying yarn, for the most part. Every now and then he brings down a bright ball and drops it at one of our feet—not with a keen, but with a familiar *auk*. Jorgie and I exchange a glance, wondering what Ben knows that we don't, marveling at his insight when one of us needs a little something extra that only he can give.

—*Kathleen R. Jorgensen*

Scratch That

Cat shows are supposed to encourage careful breeding and perfection of form . . . in the cats, that is. I've seen firsthand what trouble can happen when folks don't realize it's the animals they're meant to be judging.

I have a friend, Mrs. H, whose intuitive animal husbandry comes in an unpolished, largely educated, chubby, lower-socioeconomic package of love. Cats are her hobby, her passion, and, some might say, her obsession. She's mighty good at breeding them—maybe too good for her fellow competitors. Therein lay the problem.

A number of years back she was on top of her game. Not with her family of nine difficult kids or her abusive husband or the never-ending bills she struggled to pay on time. In general, her life was no picnic, but her cats . . . ah, perfection. They brought her a ton of joy. Her precious charges took the major prizes at every show in the area. Such was her reputation that when she was showing, some contestants just packed up and left before the judging was complete, knowing they didn't stand a chance against her. Certain members of her feline society felt downright humiliated that this woman who looked one step up from a bag lady beat them on a regular basis. It was bad enough that someone like her was allowed into their club, but her constant wins really rubbed their noses in it. To them the cats were symbols of prestige and pride—a whole lot to do with identity rather than heart.

Mrs. H didn't care for that attitude, but in her typical forgiving way she said, "To each his own." The world is big enough to let folks like that have their moment, according to her. Pity the upper-class members of her club didn't return the favor.

In a fit of jealous pique, some of them decided that Mrs. H simply wasn't up to scratch and had to go. But how to get rid of her? They couldn't just throw her out for not looking the part, not without opening a large can of legal whoop ass. So they conspired to squeeze her out with a series of cold shoulders, make her leave of her own accord.

Seems they didn't know Mrs. H very well. See, to her, anyone who doesn't talk to you is likely feeling down and in need of cheering. No matter how they snubbed her, she met their petty nastiness with her usual good heart and sunny disposition. She was just happy to be in the club, sharing her love of felines and immersing herself in all that went with loving cats.

So the snarky committee members got tougher. They changed the rules of showing several times, making it difficult for Mrs. H to come up with the entry fees and afford the new cat box decorations. She juggled her bills a little more, walked places instead of taking the bus, anything to save a few dollars so she could still enjoy her hobby.

Then one show day the snoot brigade got really dirty. We're talking that-should-be-in-a-litter-box stuff. Mrs. H had been up at dawn to groom her Persian troupe. She always did this herself, though her arthritic fingers twinged objection. Her son's friend gave her a ride to the show venue, her cat boxes filling the back of his sedan. She set up every satin drape and cat cushion with elaborate care, then petted her babies and left them while the judging took place.

She stood outside, excited and nervous, hopping from foot to foot. When the judges left and the contestants rushed back into the animal tent, she beamed at the blue champion-of-show ribbon on Big Red's cage and basked in pride for her baby boy—for about five minutes. An angry buzz of voices made her turn. Several committee members and judges stood behind her with a larger group of onlookers forming around them. One immaculately dressed, pinch-faced woman waved papers in Mrs. H's face.

"Is something wrong?" Mrs. H asked meekly, tugging the reading glasses that hung from a chain around her neck and perching them on the bridge of her nose. She read the paper, her heart jolting: *Disqualified for showing a cat that wasn't registered by closing date of applications for the show.*

"Sorry, but we need your ribbon back," a blushing judge murmured, plucking at his white coat.

The crowd behind him hushed. Either they agreed or were shocked, but the hush itself was bad enough for a shy, country-raised woman like Mrs. H.

"Big Red is registered," she stammered, pressing a trembling hand to her throat. "I know my application was a bit late. I had to raise the entry fee. I explained all that to the woman behind your desk. She didn't say anything about it being too late."

"That's just our secretary," the pinch-faced lady said as she stepped forward to snatch Mrs. H's ribbon. "She doesn't make the rules."

"But I made sure Big Red was registered in time for the show today."

"The rules do say that cats must be registered by closing date of applications, not by the time of the show," the judge murmured, staring at his shoes.

Mrs. H looked from one to the other.

The judge shrugged thin shoulders. "I'm sorry," he added, avoiding her pleading stare.

Mrs. H's big blue eyes widened and swam with tears. Then she lifted her chin, packed up her cats, and went home without another word, never realizing the worst was still to come.

About a week later, a letter arrived saying that because she'd broken the rules on the day of the show, some cat society members had moved that her yearly membership not be renewed. That was too great a blow. She fell in a messy heap on her bare wooden steps and howled for half an hour. If she couldn't show her cats, she couldn't fetch as much for her kittens, and without that income, she couldn't afford to feed all her beloved pets, not with her family situation being how it was. That meant she'd have to scale down her breeding program. And that meant selling off some of her much-adored breeders. She'd rather gnaw off her own leg.

Mrs. H wasn't the kind to drop her bundle for long. Though everything looked grim, she continued to believe that a new door would open for her. And it did, in a very unlikely place. She got a phone call from Carol, one of the fancy-dressed women she'd thought was part of the snobbish clique.

"I hate what they did to you," the five-foot-nothing fashion plate said. "Cat shows should be about our animals, not the people who own them. But if you trust me, I've got an idea how we can fix this."

Together they hatched a scheme to show the bigots the error of their ways. At the very least, it gave Mrs. H hope.

When the next cat show finally arrived, Carol entered Big Red under her name. And won, not surprisingly. Taking the blue first-prize rosette in her hand, she turned and addressed everyone present in a loud voice, "Aren't Mrs. H's cats something?"

The tent fell to awkward silence, but Carol wasn't finished. She walked over to the second-place winner and smiled, then quickly rattled off the cat's ancestry, all the way back to one of Mrs. H's cats. Then she moved on to the third-place holder and did the same.

"All of our wins are connected to Mrs. H," Carol crowed, warming to her subject. "Without her eye for genetics, the local Persian bloodlines would be nowhere near as strong. But somewhere along the line, some club members have forgotten that it's the animal's bloodlines and pedigrees we're supposed to be judging, not their owners. How is it that the woman who has done so much for us and our cats is no longer welcome in our club?"

Her face reddened with passion for her subject, even as the judges' paled with humiliation. Finally she was asked to leave—without her ribbon. The committee called an emergency meeting, and nothing more was heard from them for weeks. Then Mrs. H received another letter, this one reinstating her membership and listing all the upcoming show events. She chuckled and rubbed her double chins. She'd never been one to hold a grudge.

At the next cat show those disgruntled hoity-toities stood around in tight groups, their designer suits floating in clouds of expensive perfume. The Louis Vuitton handbags slung over elegant, gym-toned shoulders held Evian water, facial spritzer, and makeup kits for ongoing facial repairs during the day. Mrs. H, in contrast, wore her favorite cotton smock, handmade by her daughter from fabric Mrs. H had picked out at Bargain Box because she liked its cat pattern. The bodice shimmered with the gold-coated plastic and sequins of a dozen cat brooches she'd collected over the years. Her oversized vinyl pocketbook was crammed with everything imaginable for her cats' health, safety, and comfort. With her, the cats always came first. Beside her, as immaculate as ever, stood Carol, five feet of protective fury, testament to the adage, *It's not the size of the cat in the fight, it's the size of the fight in the cat*—or friend, in this case.

Mrs. H won three ribbons that day, including grand champion. Better yet, folks jostled for the chance to order her kittens, booking litters for the next year and bumping up her asking price. Every extra dollar widened her smile and ensured she'd be able to continue paying for her hobby for a long time to come.

As far as I can see, everyone won that day. Mrs. H got to keep doing what she does and loves best. The cat lines continued to improve under her clever eye. She and Carol formed a new true friendship. And a group of snobs learned that having money was no excuse for exclusive, condescending behavior toward their fellowman—bringing that cat fight, which should never have begun, to a purrrr-fect end.

—Lyndell King

Dibbs!

Having two cats is like having two children in that you must never, ever bring home something for one without buying the exact same thing for the other. Unfortunately, our cats are a bit on the spoiled side (no idea how that happened). The upshot is, even when we bring home something that is not for them, but rather for us, the cats still claim ownership.

For example, we brought home a new throw rug for the kitchen floor. Nothing fancy, just a basic woven throw with tassels on the ends. We laid it on the floor.

"What do you think?" I asked my husband.

"Looks good," he said. "I—"

A rumbling, rushing sound filled the air as two cats careened around the corner. Eyes bulging, ears laid flat, feet racing, they were neck and neck on the home stretch. Then, in a surprise move, the kitten took a Herculean leap, passing the cat, and was the first to land victoriously on the new rug.

Mrrowr! she screeched, spread-eagled across the fabric.

Rowr-rrrr! the cat yelped, looking to us as if for a judge's call. She screeched to a halt at the edge of the rug as if an invisible barrier protected it.

The kitten smirked as she pranced around the new rug.

"Well, it was nice for the thirty seconds we could call it ours," said my husband. "I'm going to watch TV."

I glared at his retreating back. Yet again, I was left to single-parent the situation. Fortunately, I had the deft touch.

"You share," I told the kitten. "Be a good kitty. Share."

The kitten's idea of sharing was to settle into the middle of the rug and begin cleaning her private parts. I decided parenting was overrated and joined my husband in front of the TV.

The kitten made herself at home, not moving for the next two hours. Our entering the kitchen didn't deter her in the least, and she went so far as to let us step over and around her as we fumbled through trying to cook and set the table.

My husband made the mistake of standing on the rug as he stirred something at the stove. A rumble emanated from deep in the kitten's throat.

"I'd move if I were you," I told him.

"Why?" he asked.

The kitten walked over and glared at the portion of his shoe on the mat.

"You're on somebody's turf," I said.

He looked down at the scowling kitten. "I pay the mortgage," he said. "If I want to stand on my new carpet, in my kitchen, no ten-pound cat is going to stop me."

I shrugged and went back to rinsing off lettuce.

The kitten nudged his ankle with her head. When subtlety didn't work, she went for an all-out head-butt.

"Hey, cut that out," said my husband.

The kitten whipped out her claws and targeted his sock, which unfortunately had his foot in it at the time.

"Ow! Hey! Ow!" He hopped off the rug.

"Us, zero. Cats, 391," I said. My husband glared at me.

The cat moped in the doorway, watching the kitten nap on the rug. But older and somewhat wiser, she was merely biding her time.

Per routine, I fed the cats at five o'clock. The cat sashayed over and planted herself in front of the kitten's dish. The kitten sat up, alarmed. The cat smiled and then sank her head deep into the kitten's food.

Rowr, rowr, psst! yelled the kitten.

My husband and I came into the kitchen.

The kitten stared accusingly at the cat. *Mrow, mow, mow!*

"Well, go get your food then," I said.

The cat hummed as she paroled the perimeter of the rug.

The kitten bit her lip and lay down on the mat.

The cat wasn't through. She started splashing around in the water dish. *Hear the water? When is the last time you went to the bathroom? Ho, hum. Splash, splash. I love playing in the runny water.*

The kitten crossed her legs. She looked worried.

Splish-splash. Splish-splash. Oh, how I love the runny, full, wet, drippy water. The kitten turned a deep shade of purple as she held her breath. Unable to bear it any longer, she tore off the carpet toward the litter box. Doing her business in record time, she raced back to the mat, coming to a dismayed stop at the edge.

The cat squatted at the corner of the rug, flipping a tassel back and forth. *Do you mind?* her expression seemed to ask the kitten. *I'm getting ready for bed. If you could just go in the other room so as not to disturb me, that would be lovely. Cheers.*

By then, I was fed up. It was impossible to get anything done in the kitchen with territorial cats nipping at my heels and with both cats toying alternatively with starvation and kidney implosion so as not to lose their claim on the rug to the other.

"We have to take action," I told my husband.

He put down the newspaper and sighed. "You're right. We've spoiled them. But with hard work and commitment on our part, I'm sure we can teach them to do better."

I stared at him. "What are you talking about?"

He stared back. "Weren't you going to lecture me that we need to find new ways of reward and discipline for the cats so as to create a fairer, more harmonious environment in which we can all learn a lesson about love and sharing?"

"What, are you on drugs?" I asked. "No. I was going to suggest we go buy two small, crappy rugs for the hall and let them duke it out there."

He thought for a moment. "Okay, that's good too.

It's really too bad we don't have kids. We'd make great parents."

—*Dena Harris*

This story was first published in Cats & Kittens *magazine, January 2004.*

The Power of the Purr

"Please, please, pul-leeze!"

My younger brother was making a good pitch for the kitten, but I could tell our mother wasn't buying it. Normally, Eddie didn't have to work this hard to get what he wanted. Complications after a tonsillectomy had kept him in the hospital for months. My parents were told he might not pull through. Now all he had to do was touch the scars on his neck and our mother would cave. But this was different; Mother hated cats.

Eddie's voice jumped another octave. He looked up, his eyes bright with tears.

Mother was a formidable opponent. Though she was all of five feet, two inches, if you counted her bun, she was much tougher than my father. She stood ramrod straight and narrowed her eyes at her young son. "You won't take care of it."

"I took good care of the fish."

"They all died."

"It wasn't my fault they ate too much."

She rolled her eyes, but I could see a slight smile forming at the corners of her mouth.

"Cats jump," she said. "It would be all over the house."

"I'll keep it in my room. I'll never ask for anything again." He rubbed his neck.

"You'll have to keep it in the basement."

I stood in awe of the master. He was only seven, but his timing was perfect.

Eddie's first-grade teacher delivered the kitten in a cardboard box. Dad played referee while we fought over the tiny fur ball. Mom must have been thinking, *What did I get myself into?* She was a calico cat, white with large patches of black and cinnamon, so of course we called her Patches. Not very original, but we were young.

Mom was true to her word. Patches was relegated to the basement with the old fish tanks and other paraphernalia of past pets.

Technically, she was Eddie's cat. But as usual, Mom was right, and he didn't take care of her. I did.

I couldn't wait for the school day to end so I could rush home and see Patches. I was a loner, and she was my new best friend and confidant—for four days. On the fifth day, she was gone.

I was at school when she launched the savage attack on my mother. It must have been brutal—for Patches. Mom claimed she was ambushed before she got to the bottom of the steps, that the laundry went flying and she barely escaped with her life. By the time my father got home, the story had been embellished many times. It was now an epic, the stuff legends are made of.

I was devastated. Dad tried to console me. "Someday you'll have your own home and all the pets you want."

"Someday" turned out to be forty-five years later, and Dad isn't around to see it. Now, I play that childhood scene in my mind like an old black-and-white movie. Maybe it's not the best memory I have of my mother, but I prefer it to the way she is today. *She should have died with Dad,* I think. Then I cringe, hating myself for thinking that way. It's not her fault she has Alzheimer's. She lives in the past now; today, I chose to follow her there.

I sigh and pick up the dishes. It's time to get a move on. I have a husband, children, a job, and two cats to take care of—as well as the woman living in my basement. I sometimes wonder how my mother, if she were aware, would feel about two cats living upstairs while she inhabits the basement. Granted, it is a lovely in-law suite, but it is still the basement.

I refused to consider the other alternative, a nursing home. My husband agreed and willingly accepted my ailing mother into our already chaotic household. Luckily, I am married to a patient man. When I met John, I had three children and a dog. He adjusted to our hectic lifestyle quickly. When the dog had to be put to sleep, he was the one who suggested another pet.

John wanted another dog. I wanted a cat. He claimed he wasn't a cat person. I told him he could change. Round and round we went. The deciding factor was work. No one was home during the day to walk a dog. Secretly, I felt I had worn him down; my brother taught me well.

We were confused. There were so many different cat breeds. I was partial to the old-style Siamese, with their athletic bodies, round heads, and blue eyes. And I loved the striking contrast between the body color and the darker points that characterized the breed. Most of the Siamese we saw were slender and elegant, modern cats with wedge-shaped heads. They were beautiful but not what I wanted.

We were directed to a breeder who also raised Tonkinese cats. She was expecting a litter and promised to give us first pick when they were old enough. My husband was still a little hesitant, but he agreed to come back.

Two months later we returned and were assaulted by bouncing brown-and-white Tribbles, full of kinetic energy. Three were pointed. Their little bodies were white but would darken as they got older. John put the tiny girl on his lap. She climbed up his chest and draped herself around his neck like a mink collar. He was smitten. I held the two boys. They were identical in every way. One looked me in the eye and revved up his motor. Okay, we'll take two.

I believed that two cats would be good company for each other, but I feared they would bond and ignore us. I couldn't have been more wrong. Oh, Buffy and Spike were inseparable all right. They slept together, curling their little bodies into a perfect circle like yin and yang. They ate together, sometimes out of the same bowl. And they groomed each other incessantly. They were squeaky clean, a fact we could attest to by the number of hairballs we stepped on.

But whoever said cats are not pack animals was dead wrong. Our bed was their bed. When John and I left in the morning, they'd see us off. At 4:00 P.M., they'd be sitting by the door, tails erect, waiting to greet us. They turned up their noses at table scraps but sat patiently at our feet while we ate dinner. And try to read the paper: forget about it. Spike would plant himself on top of it and nudge his head under my hand, as if to say, *You've been gone all day, pay attention to me.*

Spike was the conversationalist. I learned to differentiate his meows and appreciate his nonstop purring. Buffy was the little princess, quiet and aloof. When she went belly-up for me, I was amazed. That was high praise from her. She was telling me *I trust you.* But when it came time to cut her nails, welcome to my nightmare. I'd chase her around the house, clippers in hand, while she played Freddy Krueger. Good thing I don't scare easy.

John couldn't remember why he wanted a dog. Our cats came when called, played fetch, and never needed to be walked. They were perfect.

In fact, my life was pretty much perfect—until the day my husband and brother carried my mother into our house. She looked so frail, nothing like the mother I once knew. Her neat cotton dress had given way to baggy sweats, because they were easy to get on and off. She had always taken great pride in her hair. As a child I watched her put it up, amazed at the number of bobby pins that disappeared into the thick bun. It was painful to see it hanging long and unkempt over her shoulders. Her feisty personality was gone. She was a shell of her old self, completely dependent and relegated to a wheelchair in our basement, her own private death row.

We had no idea how she would react to Buffy and Spike, and I had no desire to find out. I felt it best to keep them separated. The caretakers were instructed to make sure the basement door stayed closed.

It is said that curiosity killed the cat, but Buffy and Spike were willing to take that risk. The locked door became an obsession. They took to hanging around, waiting for an opportunity to scoot through. Their big chance finally came. One day I wasn't quick enough in closing the door, and down they went. I followed in a panic. Mom was parked in front of the television. In the background, Lawrence Welk was saying, "Wunnerful, wunnerful" in his thick German accent.

Spike took a flying leap and landed on the adjustable table over her lap.

"Oh, no!" My heart leaped, but my mother didn't move.

"Mew." It was Spike's plea for attention. He looked her in the face as if to say, *Cat got your tongue?*

No reaction. At least she didn't seem frightened. Curious to see what would happen, I didn't interfere.

"Meow!" Now it was a command. Still no response.

Spike declared a cease-fire. He waved his tail in the air like a white flag and lay down on the table. Was he giving up? No way. He started his motor, a tactic that never failed to elicit a stroke from his adoring humans, and prodded her hand with his nose. No response. He made himself comfortable; he would stick around anyway. What harm could it do? I left them and went upstairs.

After that, I got in the habit of leaving the door open. Every day, Spike would sit on the table purring. And every day my mother would ignore him. Did she know he was there? I thought not. Buffy slept nearby on the floor. It was beneath her to work that hard for attention.

A few months passed. One day Spike didn't greet me after work. The caretaker met me at the bottom of the stairs, a finger over her lips. Smiling, she pointed. There was my boy on the table . . . with my mother's hand resting on his head.

Guilt flooded me. Communicating with my mother had become so frustrating that I'd stopped making the effort. I fed her, bathed her, diapered her, and then disappeared. Spike knew better. He never gave up on her.

The vibrations of his strong, soothing purr must have gotten through to her. He taught me how a comforting presence and a soft touch can work miracles. Thanks to him, there was still time for me to connect with my mother. And thanks to the power of the purr, my mother became a cat lover.

—*Gail Pruszkowski*

Cat People

Cat people are weird. At least that's what dog people say. Well, they don't say it to your face, but they think it. You see, I used to run with dog people. In fact, I was raised in a dog-people home. That's where I first learned the rules—dog people are mellow and easygoing like their animals, and cat people are uptight, finicky, mercurial, and, well, catlike. This impression influenced me to such a degree that I hardly paid attention to a cat for the first forty-three years of my life.

When my husband and I moved several years ago (with our dog), we joined a local church and began to make new friends through a home Bible study. Our hosts were what you might label the bookish type. They were undeniably bright, well-read academics with a penchant for dissecting and analyzing Old Testament passages. They were so well versed in all things intellectual that I quickly felt like a simpleton in their presence. My only chance at keeping my head above water might have been in a game of Trivial Pursuit, were I to draw the entertainment category. Given the chance, I probably could cancel out their Ivy League educations with my extensive knowledge of "Hit Sitcoms of the Seventies." Anyway, they were really smart college professors who talked a lot about their cat, hence solidifying my preconceived notion of the cat person. It's not that their tales about Scooter weren't mildly interesting; it's just that nothing they shared could compete with the amount of enthusiasm with which it was imparted. They practically would faint with excitement over his most recent antics, only to be met with a mere cordial reception by their audience. *Cat people,* I thought with disdain.

Our dog died last year. We loved her so much that I couldn't even think about bringing another dog into our home. This, however, did not stop my children from campaigning for a puppy. They were full of empty promises to train, bathe, feed, and walk the hoped-for, begged-for new dog. It was obvious our house felt empty without Daisy, but I just wasn't ready.

One day we were at our local pet store getting food for Lola, the goldfish, when my son noticed several cages filled with adult cats and some kittens.

The Animal Rescue League was visiting and inviting people to adopt a cat.

"Mom! Mom! Look!" my kids exclaimed. "Kittens! Can we get one? Can we? Can we? Huh, Mom? Awww, they're so cute! Look, Mom, look!"

"I see them," I replied. "And they are very cute, but you guys have never even mentioned getting a cat. You just want a cat because we are here right now. What happened to the puppy campaign?"

They quickly grew silent as we agreed to stay for ten minutes to admire the cats, make a donation, and be on our way. My daughter was skipping from cage to cage, remarking on their different colorings. I was admiring the mother cats from a distance—those poor mommy cats, found in alleyways with litters of mouths to feed.

My son, however, was experiencing something far different. Crouched on the floor at the very end of a long row of cages, he sat holding the paw of one sprightly, engaging, six-month-old kitten named Diego. Each time he wiggled his fingers through the cage, Diego would answer with his paw, curling it around my son's fingers, as if beckoning him to come closer. They were, in essence, holding hands, and Diego would not leave my son's side. A volunteer noticed this bond immediately and offered to let Diego out for a visit. I reluctantly agreed. My thoughts were racing. *What am I doing? We don't want a cat. We don't ever even talk about cats. Oh my gosh, look at that adorable cat in my son's lap.*

Slowly, my daughter approached Diego. As with my son, he reached for her with his snowy white paw. She scooted closer, and Diego curled up in her lap. I sat on the floor near my children, and we were silent in unison. We were a captivated audience, beholden to this creature, utterly smitten and charmed. He purred with delight at the slightest touch, nestling his head in our hands, directing our strokes, lifting his chin, as if he were smiling. We left the store with a new family member. He explored the house for five minutes and assumed his rightful place. There was no adjustment period, nothing tentative. Diego had simply come home.

It has been five months now. To say we are all in love with Diego is an understatement. We wait anxiously for him to choose one of us as we gather to watch a television program. Who will be the lucky one to have Diego sit in his lap? We argue over which is his favorite toy and who can coax him to spring the highest after a feather on a string. We call each other to come have a look at him during one of his sun baths, sharing our admiration for his luxurious poses—twisted and contorted so as to match a particular patch of sun. We laugh uproariously at his antics, like the time he shot down the hallway like a bullet, bounding from the couch to the air hockey table and across the living room again, landing in a bowl of popcorn. We wave at him from the car as he perches atop the desk that sits under the front window, his paw pressed against the glass. We feel a tinge of sadness driving away and often cushion our remorse with lively discussions of how Diego might pass the time in our absence. My daughter imagines he drives around in her Barbie Bus, while my son envisions him logging on to Wikipedia or reading the newspaper.

These things may seem unlikely, but then you don't know our dear Diego, who frequently serenades us with piano concertos. Once we are all sleeping soundly and the house is sufficiently hushed, Diego will delicately walk across the keys with his nimble paws, striking a dissonant yet somehow soothing combination of chords. They echo throughout the house and gently ring in our ears like a grandfather clock, reminding us all that someone is keeping watch and all is well. Then he roams into corners unexplored before curling up with the lucky someone who will slumber next to his purring lullaby.

I was catching up with an old friend on the phone recently. She asked if anything was new. I couldn't wait to tell her about Diego. As I attempted to convey the utter joy this curious creature has brought into our lives, I suddenly realized it was falling on deaf ears. My excitement over his numerous talents seemed rather frenetic against the backdrop of adult conversation—

like a child recalling a trip to Grandma's house or Disneyland. I finally gave up and changed the subject, yet I was left with a residual angst. *How could someone not understand how delightful Diego is? How could they not appreciate his mischievous ways, his boundless affection, his uncanny sense of timing? Why, it's preposterous that one could not be forever intrigued by this irrepressible creature.* That's when it hit me. *Oh my goodness, I realized, I am a cat person. I have become a full-fledged cat person. What's next? Will I be one of those middle-aged women wearing cat pins and cat earrings, drinking my coffee from a cat mug? How long before I am attending cat conventions and subscribing to* Cat Fancy? *I'm the little old lady in apartment 9.*

Truth be told, there will always be cats to comfort lonely souls who no one else can. The little old lady in apartment 9 is actually in good company. Surely, her library is filled with Hemingway, who was a notorious cat lover. I love the photo of him in Key West. He sits among his weathered furniture with books and manuscripts scattered about, feeding one of several cats perched in various places. Did one of them ever drape themselves across his notebook as he wrote? Then there is T. S. Eliot. Now, we cat people have artful poetry with which to describe our indescribable friends. ("He is more of a Rum Tum Tugger type, definitely not a Mr. Mistoffelees.") And, of course, we have each other. Cat people find each other and make up for all those lonely, lopsided conversations with noncat people. We affirm our mutual observations with a knowing smile or a comparable story, but more important, we appreciate the mystery of it all. Cats are full of surprises, and we secretly envy them. Wouldn't we all love to change on a whim as they do? To be loyal, yes, but master of all our persuasions, never questioning our position or stance.

A few days ago my kids and I got stuck in a traffic jam on the way to basketball practice. My son was very anxious that we would be late, and my daughter wouldn't stop complaining.

"Why don't we sing?" I suggested. "It always helps to pass the time."

"I want to choose the song!" yelled my daughter.

The car grew quiet as we waited for her to begin.

"There was a farmer had a cat, and Diego was his name-o. D-i-e-g-o, D-i-e-g-o, D-i-e-g-o, and Diego was his name-o. . . ."

We inched our way to practice singing at the top of our lungs. I wasn't certain we would be there on time, but I was very confident of one thing along the way—we are cat people through and through. There's no turning back now. But who would want to?

—*Shawn Daywalt Lutz*

My Life as the Other Woman

My daughter, Alice, traveled home to be with her dad on his sixty-third birthday, carrying his birthday present close to her chest. She entered the family room, where he now spent his days confined to a battery-operated reclining chair. Peeping out from just above her arms were the frightened eyes and furry ears of a very young, very tiny, black-and-white kitten.

"Happy birthday, Dad." She grinned, plopping the furry ball into his lap as she leaned in to kiss him.

I'm not sure which of us was more startled, my husband, Richard, or me. I glared at Alice. The last thing in the world we needed in our lives at this time was an animal to take care of. Richard was still coming to terms with the reality of his continuing decline and the terminal cancer that would claim him in the end. *Why me?* was written on his face as he sat, day after day, staring into space, feeling powerless and useless. The birthday present trembling on his lap went unacknowledged.

Later, out of earshot of her dad, I pointed out to Alice the inappropriateness of her gift.

"Mom, don't you keep up with the research?" was her reply. "Animals are very therapeutic for shut-ins. Nursing homes use them all the time."

I wasn't impressed with the comparison. She would be gone after the weekend, while we would still have the kitten. Before leaving for work, I always placed Richard's pills, liquids, and lunch on the table beside his chair. What if the cat knocked them down after I'd gone? I left the walker within easy reach for his trips to the bathroom. What if the kitten tumbled under foot when he rose and tripped him? Alice dismissed my fears and said I worried too much.

We went through the motions of a happy birthday dinner. Richard managed a weak smile as we helped him blow out the candle on his cake. I tried to draw his attention to the kitten by asking for a name. He didn't answer.

"Her name is Lincoln," Alice said, and Richard laughed.

She was referring to her father's fascination with our sixteenth president. Richard loved history, and the last meaningful piece of research he had been able to complete was for a soon-to-be-published piece on Abraham Lincoln. Its acceptance had brought him great satisfaction.

Lincoln is an odd name for a cat, especially a female one, but no other suggestions were made, so the name stuck. And at least it had made Richard laugh.

Later, Alice went out to spend her last evening home with friends before leaving for the airport, and Richard and I settled in to watch our Sunday night television shows, he in his chair with the cat on his lap, I on the couch nearby. Halfway into the second-hour show, the kitten began to shake violently, then convulse. I located a twenty-four-hour emergency veterinarian service in the phone book, wrapped little Lincoln in a bath towel, and raced out to seek help.

The veterinarian was not optimistic. He said the kitten had been left at the animal shelter at too young an age and had caught an illness she might not have the strength to withstand. The next seventy-two hours would determine her fate. If she could survive that long, she would make it. However, the kitten would need frequent medication, administered through an eyedropper. It was too late to return her to the shelter; they would not accept a critically ill animal. I put the medicine in my purse, paid the bill, and drove home with Lincoln, now stabilized and no longer convulsing but still a very sick cat.

I gave Richard the grim prognosis and said I would arrange to take the next couple of days off from work. His response surprised me. He reached out for the towel-wrapped kitten still in my arms. "I can take care of her. You don't have to stay home," he said. It was the first time in many weeks that he had shown an interest in anything.

I placed Lincoln back on his lap and handed him the medicine bottle, explaining the frequency and size of the doses she needed. He nodded, carefully removing the dropper, checking its fullness, and gently coaxing it into the kitten's mouth. That done, he went back to watching television, interrupting his focus only when it was time to medicate his patient again.

I was consumed with dread the next day, worrying about what I would find when I returned. *I shouldn't have left*, I told myself. Yet Richard had wanted to take care of the cat, and not to have let him try would have further diminished him. I raced home, hoping I'd done the right thing. I entered as quietly as I could and headed toward the family room. I stopped short and stood in the archway unobserved as I took in the scene.

Richard was once more coaxing the medication into the kitten's mouth, speaking encouragement to her as he worked. "You're going to make it, Lincoln, don't you worry. I'm not going to let you die. You're going to get well."

I retreated back outside, wiped my tears, took a deep breath and reopened the door, closing it more loudly this time. "I'm home," I called, and strode into the family room. "How are my patients doing today?"

Richard smiled up at me. "We're okay. How was your day?"

He hadn't asked me that in a long time. Something had changed. Fighting to keep the kitten alive had brought him back to life. Alice had been right; Lincoln was excellent therapy for her dad. The kitten gave him purpose again. But even Alice could not have predicted what happened next.

As Lincoln grew stronger, so did the bond between man and cat. All our previous pets had gravitated to me, the lady who filled the food dish. Not Lincoln. She was Richard's, and he was hers. Where did this leave me? I was soon to find out.

Lincoln grew into a healthy cat. Her antics amused Richard and kept him entertained. Even when off his lap, she stayed close, keeping an eye on him. As she grew stronger and he grew weaker, their roles seemed to reverse. If she sensed a sadness coming over him, she returned to his lap, nuzzled her head under his chin before settling down, knowing how stroking her soft coat could calm him. She knew how to make her man happy, and Richard was her man. I was seen as the other woman.

I was reminded of this daily in many ways, some more deadly than others. At first, it was the get-your-hands-off-my-man-you-hussy message I got whenever I leaned over to kiss my husband, and a paw would come up beside my face, claws extended, to plant a slap upon my cheek as my lips touched Richard's.

My troubles multiplied when it was time to sleep. I'd get Richard into bed and snuggle in beside him, but not for long. Suddenly Lincoln was in the bed too, plopping herself down between our heads, biting my face and pushing me until I inched farther away and she could settle in between our heads.

I wasn't getting the message, though, and clearly stronger measures were needed if Lincoln was to succeed in removing me from the picture. Ambush was her next tactic of choice. I learned to look around corners when approaching a room or hallway, but I was never quick enough. She always knew when and where I was coming into range and would leap out from behind the nearest wall to bite my ankles or grab my nylons with her sharpened claws.

Ruined stockings and bloody, scratched legs didn't seem to dissuade me either. I continued to come home from work, and worse yet, I continued to greet Richard with a kiss, in spite of the furry interference. This was more than Lincoln could stand. She became more sinister in her plotting.

When Richard became too ill to climb stairs, we re-arranged where we slept, but his study and much of our clothes and other items remained where they were. If either of us needed something, I'd go get it. It was still dark out when I would go upstairs in the mornings to dress for work. I didn't turn the hall light on going up or down, because I didn't want to wake Richard before I had to. Lincoln realized that if she hid her white paws under her and flattened her black body against the dark carpet of the next stair in my descent, I could easily be tripped, tumble down the long staircase, and break my neck. Once the undertakers left with my body, she'd have Richard all to herself.

She nearly succeeded. I took many a stumble when my foot hit and slid from her back, but a quick grip of the banister always helped me regain my balance. Surprisingly enough, she never gnawed at the banister's slats to make the railing too weak to hold my weight. At least, not that I know of.

Sadly, we both lost him in the end. Shortly after Richard died and there was just the two of us alone in the house, Lincoln went out and never returned. Perhaps she went looking for her man. In any case, she had no desire to live there with me. I wished she would have stayed. I missed that jealous, homicidal cat.

—Marcia Rudoff

Cat Prints on the Volvo

There are times in life when reason, despite all of its, well, reasonableness, loses out to something more abstract. Call it pure emotional response, if you will, but I prefer to think of it as spontaneous affirmation of life—or just saying "Yes" when logically one should say "Keep walking."

It's not like I woke up one morning and said to my family, "I think we should get a cat today." Instead, it was evening when the cat found us, as some of the best pets do. My son and I were taking a walk around the neighborhood, as we often did before he got too old for that to be cool. We climbed the hill up to a small stretch of unpaved road where there was a no-through street and lots of trees.

From the corner of my eye I spied a miniature mess, a feline foundling. He was an average black-

and-white shorthair with the requisite white paws to match. Hunched on the far side of a puddle, he was wet and bedraggled from the first rains of autumn. His stark green eyes requested mercy, and the look was accompanied by the pitiful *meow* of a creature who was tired of mousing for survival when most animals of his kind could be found contentedly crunching Friskies in someone's sunny mud room.

"Just keep walking," I said to my son.

Oh, don't get me wrong. I adore cats. In fact, I was still healing from the loss of my twenty-year-old cat, who had seen me grow up from a dreamy poet/waitress to a mother of two and now a new step-mother of two. That type of loyal companionship is not easily replaced.

But I'd learned my lesson about animal rescue the hard way. While in college, my friends and I would adopt stray cats and then struggle to pay the unanticipated veterinary bills. Roommates would bring the "alley cat from behind the restaurant" home only to have it run away from unconscious youthful neglect. After too many of those botched rescue missions, I'd learned to keep my eyes on the road and walk faster when a stray tried desperately to latch on.

Despite my cool and detached demeanor, the kitten quickly analyzed me as a long-dormant sucker. *Meow-rrrrow, meow, mew* . . . it followed us down the hill, past the first block and almost to the stop sign.

"Just ignore it," I firmly advised my son.

He kept looking back. Finally he stopped and stood in the middle of the sidewalk, hands on hips. Then he turned to me and said with a firm tenderness, "Mom, it's obvious he's sending out a rescue signal."

That did it. My heart, so carefully folded shut, broke open.

"Yes, I believe he is." I scooped up the stray and turned my sweatshirt up like the kitten rescue sling it was obviously meant to be.

When we entered the house, all the other children crowded around. "Can we keep him, can we, can we?" they begged. So great was the excitement that my fifteen-year-old valiantly offered to skip soccer practice that evening to care for him.

"This is an exceptional situation, Mom. I'm sure Coach would understand."

"Um, I think not, but the cat will be here when you get back."

There was the small matter of convincing my logical new husband about the obvious benefits of this unexpected adoption. Weren't we already struggling to adapt to the newness of our marriage, the blending of the families? What about the added expense of a pet? My husband is a no-nonsense guy. I wasn't sure this was going to meet with his approval. Oh, but this was the first lesson, among many, that the kitten would teach me. It turned out my husband could be just as much a pushover as I was for a fur ball in need of shelter.

The name for the cat was voted "Boots," despite its utter lack of originality. The name was *easy*. Given all the new challenges of learning about getting along together as a family, we needed easy!

Boots became an unlikely liaison, an ambassador for family unity. He didn't play favorites. He could be found lazing on any of our five beds. He leapt indiscriminately on any lap that would have him. Everyone wanted to feed him, find him, play catch-the-catnip-mouse on a string with him, and talk about how funny he was. All the simplest things that bring joy into a home, Boots seemed to represent. Boots taught by example: *Relax, you don't have to try so hard.*

The first time my new mother-in-law came to visit from out of town, there was a bit of a lull in the conversation. Just then Boots trotted into the middle of the room and licked his paw. Suddenly, we were leaning in, swapping stories about her many Siamese cats and talking about how cats could easily rule the planet if they wanted to.

The lessons of Boots were at times humbling. Our first Christmas, the entire family went out to chop a tree and, instead of agreeing on one, we argued for an hour about whether we should get a traditional scotch pine, like "we" had always gotten, or a noble fir, like "they" always had. We compromised with a plain fir. In the end, Boots reminded us that none of this mattered when he brought the fully decorated tree crashing to the floor after trying to catch the singing bird on the top.

Boots liked to go sit out on the top of my car at night and look at the moon. I'd bought that used Volvo with the notion of trying to "upgrade my ride," but also because it was a logical and safe choice for the family. Despite my efforts to keep it clean and in good soccer-mom style, I'd usually wake up in the morning to find cat prints all over it. Ah, lesson learned: get over yourself already!

After almost a year together, all the boys lobbied hard for us to get a dog. Never in my life would it have occurred to me that a three-month-old puppy could push Boots out of the house, but that is precisely what happened. Within a few days of getting the puppy, Boots, visibly upset, vanished.

Despite lost cat signs and searches, we never saw Boots again. Everyone took the loss of Boots very hard. In an attempt to soothe scratches on hearts that were having trouble healing, I found myself saying, "Maybe he had a mission, and his mission was completed." Boots brought us closer as a family. He was a teacher and a healer who just happened to love licking the bottom of tuna can.

I really do believe Boots had the charm and wherewithal to find a new home for himself. He certainly knew how to charm the logic out of me. The rational side of me understands that letting go when you're not ready is a part of life; it's the irrational side that rescued that little kitten and rejoiced in giving him a home and now mourns his absence. Occasionally, when I go out to get the newspaper in the morning, I glance over at the car and imagine cat prints, smudged like little hearts, running up and down the Volvo.

—Elizabeth King Gerlach

True Love

Love is patient,
Love is kind
And is not jealous;
Love does not brag
And is not arrogant . . .

—*1 Corinthians 13.4*

When the minister read this biblical passage at my sister's wedding in 1987, it occurred to me that very few people have that special love, including my parents. Mom and Dad, or, as most of the world knows them, Evelynne and Norman Smith, had few shared interests aside from us four kids, and we had all grown up and moved out. It seemed that they'd never found true love.

Twenty years later, my parents still had little in common, except for daily medications and frequent medical appointments. Dad, eighty-four, spent time on the computer and napping, while Mom, nine years younger, watched television, read, and challenged herself with crossword puzzles. They shared meals, and otherwise either bickered or ignored each other.

With no one else in the house and Dad's poor hearing, I imagined a typical day going something like this:

"GOOD MORNING, NORM."

"Beg your pardon?"

"I SAID, 'GOOD MORNING.'"

"Oh."

Then, fifteen hours later:

"GOODNIGHT, NORM"

"Beg your pardon?"

"I SAID, 'GOODNIGHT.'"

With not much in between, besides:

"DO YOU WANT MORE SOUP?"

"Beg your pardon?"

"I SAID, 'DO YOU WANT MORE SOUP?'"

You get the idea.

Then, on an ordinary September afternoon last year, my parents, in their fifty-seventh year of marriage, discovered true love.

The day started as any other: Mom up at 7:00, Dad at 8:00, in time for his handful of medications and the breakfast Mom set out for him. Finishing lunch around 11:45, Mom peeled her apple and remarked, "The Granny Smiths haven't been very good lately," to anyone who might hear her. No one did.

Dad had just returned from scaling a mountain during WW II in his nap, and Mom was helping Sue Grafton solve a mystery from her love seat when the back door opened and in stepped my sister Marla and her daughter Jayme. Jayme held a pet carrier containing a pint-sized ginger tabby named Hubert.

"We were so surprised!" Mom told me three months later as we sat in her kitchen at Christmas. "Then we wondered how Hubert would adjust to living with us, but you can see he fits right in."

I chuckled as my eyes took in the furry mice strewn about the floor, the blue cloths protecting every good chair, and the living room table with two small plants pushed into a corner so Hubert could have an unobstructed view of outside.

"Mom," I laughed, "I think you've fit into his routine!" Mom sheepishly agreed.

Marla and Jayme had planned for a long time to give Mom and Dad a pet. The perfect opportunity arose when Hubert wasn't getting along with the other two cats in the house and Marla remembered that he and Dad were real buddies when my dad had visited. The solution was a stroke of genius, perhaps a match made in heaven.

Now, at Mom and Dad's home the mundane is entertaining. Hubert has breakfast at 7:00, like Mom, and supper at 4:30 when Mom and Dad eat theirs. You can set your watch by him: When it's snack time at 11:00 A.M. and again at 8:00 P.M., he leads or follows Dad until they arrive at the treat drawer.

The little cat gets involved in all activities in the house. First thing in the morning, he leads Mom to her treadmill in the basement. When he tires of watching, he scampers back upstairs, returning at the precise time she finishes.

As Dad eats breakfast, Hubert sits on the table by his cereal bowl, but only if Mom is still on her treadmill. Then Dad makes his slow way down to his computer with Hubert walking ahead of him. In Dad's office, Hubert curls up under a cabinet or on some high perch. His favorite game involves running along the computer hutch above Dad and sending precious mementoes flying in all directions. Dad's quiet office has never seen such excitement.

Hubert has even adopted some of Mom and Dad's habits. Recently, as the three of them returned from a visit to the vet, Dad hit the bathroom, Mom waited her turn, and Hubert headed down to the litter box.

Because I live two provinces away, I heard about Hubert long before I met him. In our weekly phone calls, Dad's favorite topic used to be the weather. Now when I ask, "How's Hubert?" either of my parents can talk nonstop for ten minutes!

Phone calls are also often interrupted, like when Mom calls out, "Norm, what's Hubert got?" or Dad exclaims excitedly, "There's my kitty!" as I'm bragging about his granddaughters' exploits. Dad keeps me up-to-date on the latest round of "bite the foot," in which Hubert nips, paws, and bites Dad's socked feet, while Dad loudly encourages him and laughs uproariously—even when blood is drawn.

When I finally met Hubert at Christmas, I was struck by how affectionate he is. He loves people—runs to see who's at the door whenever there's a knock and narrows his eyes with pleasure when he's being petted or held. If you're headed somewhere, he'll get in front of you, especially if you're on stairs, and plop down on his back so that you just have to scratch his tummy before you can proceed. My parents have come close to tripping on this feisty feline, but they never get angry at him.

While my daughters stacked presents around the little Christmas tree clamped tightly to Hubert's plant table, Mom urged Dad to get his camera. On his return, Steph and Maddie posed, presents in hands, smiles on faces. Dad started to focus, but then said, "Wait! Where's Hubert?"

Mom left the room, calling out, "Hubert! Hubert Smith!" She returned shortly with the happy cat lounging contentedly in her arms. The girls embraced Hubert, and the picture was taken.

Photographs of Hubert gazing wisely into space grace my parent's refrigerator and the kitchen wall as well as Dad's desk. Mom has only one photo in her bedroom—of Hubert with that same wise gaze.

My mother speaks to Hubert in a baby-talk voice, referring to herself and Dad as "Momma" and "Dad." Dad's "Hubert voice" is one I haven't heard since I was a small child in need of discipline, a mock-angry voice good-naturedly scolding the cat with, "No, no, no!"

"Your father spoils Hubert worse than anyone," Mom confides.

A while ago Dad had the flu and only Mom spoke in our weekly call. "Dad will be up and about soon," she said. "Hubert keeps us going."

And he does. Knowing the little cat is depending on them to feed and care for him launches Mom and Dad out of bed in the morning. When Mom returns from the bathroom in the night, she knows Hubert will be lying on her floor. She can't see him in the dark, so she carefully makes her way, and when she comes to the waiting cat, she picks him up, kisses his soft forehead, and then gently puts him out of the room and closes the door. She has learned that his nighttime antics will keep her awake if he's allowed to stay in her room.

Recently Mom visited us in Alberta. Dad chose to stay home "with Hubert," and the two of them did just fine. "He's perfect company," Dad says.

My elderly father and his two-year-old cat delight in many of the same pastimes, including napping in the sun like old dogs. Hubert also enjoys being up high—say, on the fridge—and exploring territory "where no cat has gone before." I tell Dad that Hubert is like him, because Dad was a paratrooper and commando in World War II and Hubert is just as brave and foolhardy. This makes Dad smile.

Hubert doesn't have meltdowns or mood swings, and even though Mom and Dad swear he talks to them, he never talks back. He's excited by birds outside the window, food in his dish, and strangers knocking on the door. He brings a smile to your face, even if a moment earlier you were irritated or sad. And when you're holding him and you're both warm and content, you feel like the luckiest person in the world.

Love and laughter fill my parents' home again. There are kisses and caresses and soft words. No one could have predicted that, at this point in their lives, true love would find them. And it's all because of one of God's small creatures.

I believe in angels. I am convinced they are sent to us when we need them most. I can even say that I've met an angel or two, including one whom my Dad calls his "tender little kitten."

> *Love is patient,*
> *Love is kind*
> *And is not jealous;*
> *Love does not brag*
> *And is not arrogant . . .*

Hubert has shown us love in the truest sense of the word.

—Julie F. Smith

Wild Thing, You Moved Me

We heard a rustling in the woods but couldn't see anything. My husband and I stopped to listen, wondering what it could be. Through the tangled bush, off the side of the hiking trail on our North Georgia mountain farm, we finally spotted a beautiful, brown-mottled cat munching on a bird. Feathers were dripping from her mouth and whiskers—just like the cats you see in cartoons. Then, to our surprise, we heard a kitten's meow, and a tiny gray tabby with gold eyes came out from the underbrush. Unafraid, the kitten came right up to us, but the mother cat ran away.

I stooped to pick her up and nestled her under my chin. Her soft face rubbed against my cheek.

"Isn't she sweet?" I said.

My husband agreed. I think he loves cats more than I do.

"Look, hon," I said, "she's got six toes, like the Hemingway cats."

"They look like little mittens," he said.

"We have to keep her. Can we, please?"

"Sure, but what do you think Figuero will do when we bring her home? He's had the run of the house for years. And what about the dog, having to deal with another cat?"

"Everyone will have to adjust," I said. "She's coming home with us. Her six toes must represent a good omen, don't you think?"

After much deliberation, we decided to name her after the 1968 classic tune by Tommy James and the Shondells, "Mony Mony." At home, Figuero, our super-fat, laid-back, black-and-white cat tolerated Mony's playfulness. Our border collie, Ruby, knew to stay back from Mony's lightning-fast swats.

As Mony grew, however, her feral ways returned. Though I didn't understand what was going on with her, I knew she was miserable. She wouldn't let us come near her, and when we did get close enough to touch her, she hissed. Her attitude got so bad that we gave her the nickname "Meany Mony."

After being hissed at one too many times, my husband said, "Don't you think we should bring her back up to the farm where she came from? She probably will be much happier there."

I nodded in agreement. "Yes, she's not at all happy as a city cat. Besides, she would have the barn for protection, and I believe she is quite capable of taking care of herself."

I bought her a feeder that would hold enough food to carry her through the week. We left her with much trepidation, hoping and praying she would be okay. Sure enough, all went well. Actually, she not only got by, she thrived. Her whole demeanor changed. She started loving on us again. Upon our weekend arrivals, even before the car door would slam shut, we could hear her coming to greet us, meowing her hellos with each step.

After a while, we had more trails cut through our property. On the hilly part, we have two good miles of paths. Hiking the steep terrain helps keep us in shape. Our border collie loves to hike as much as we do. She bounds ahead of us, looking back constantly to make sure we are following her. We can even hike through the summer, if we get out early in the day before it heats up too much.

One day, we had another tag-along. Behind us we heard Mony's telltale meow walk, just like she does when she comes to greet us. We were amazed that she wanted to hike with us, and we thought for sure she would turn back. But she didn't. She stuck it out for the entire hike. Now she follows us regularly when we go on our walks.

One summer day, we let too much of the morning slip by before we started on our trek. We soon realized we should have waited until the next day. Sweat pouring off our brows, we looked back and saw poor Mony still behind us, panting, with her ears bright pink. A real trooper, she never stopped to rest. Now that's some cat, a dedicated hiker, through and through.

When I think of Mony, the hiking cat, she gives me hope for the dream my husband and I have for our property. We want to start a tree farm and grow pesticide-free vegetables for our community. We hope to get involved with Community Supported Agriculture (CSA), whereby people would sign up to receive a portion of our crops on a weekly basis, and to also provide fresh produce to local farmer's markets.

Who are we, one might ask, to think we can become farmers at midlife? But to us, becoming farmers is like the cat becoming a hiker.

My husband has been a corporate executive for eighteen years, and I've been a stay-at-home mom. Like Mony, who was miserable in the city, my husband has become extremely uncomfortable with corporate life. On top of being unhappy at work, the daily four-hour commute downtown makes it even harder to face each day. Since we bought our farm property, he lives for the weekends. He loves working outside. When he's in the great outdoors, growing and building things, he feels like he's in his element. I love being his helpmate, too. Although hard work can be a challenge, it totes great rewards—one of the biggies, stress relief. As his work downtown trudges on, worry etches lines in my husband's face. Spending time at the farm erases those lines.

Mony Mony has taught me a thing or two. She has shown me that when we leave an environment that makes us uncomfortable and go to a place where we feel at home, we can flourish. We can accomplish things that are out of the ordinary for us—things that surprise others. If we're in our element, we can be successful at whatever we put our minds to—even if the effort causes our tongues to hang out and our ears to turn red. Thanks, Mony Mony, for inspiring us to reach for our dreams.

—*Susan M. Schulz*

Ozzie to the Rescue

The headache had started the night before. By the time my two-and-a-half-year-old son, Nathaniel, had awakened from his afternoon nap, I was shivering with fever and barely able to stand upright.

"Oh, honey, be a good boy until Daddy comes home." I handed him an opened box of Cheerios and a sipper cup of milk. "Maybe there is something worthwhile on PBS."

Literally crawling to the television, I fired it up under the watchful eye of our youthful and recently rescued-from-the-animal shelter tuxedo, Oz. Although my husband, Art, had grown up in a house full of cats, Ozzie was my first feline experience. In fact, I considered myself a dog lover, and influenced by my mother's belief in the old wives' tale that cats were dirty, unruly beasts that sucked the breath out of little, helpless babies, I hadn't really wanted to get a moggy at all. Of course, logically, I dismissed my mother's archaic view of cats. But deep inside, I secretly had my doubts. As a result, I'd formed no warm, fuzzy camaraderie with our new addition. Quite simply, I didn't trust him.

Now, the agile young tom leaped silently onto the TV set, his nose twitching at my odd scent. He batted playfully at my hand as I flipped the dial in search of an educational program. But, as usual, I brushed him away. Not that it mattered; at this point, I was too weak and ailing to care about the cat or to explore the channels for long. I soon gave up, content to let some mindless cartoons rot Nathaniel's impressionable young mind, while I, wrapped in an afghan, collapsed, shivering, onto the floor's heating vent.

With my son settled, I alternately prayed I'd get warm before I died and that Art would get home soon. My face hurt so badly that I could scarcely see straight. Knifelike pains shot through my eyeballs every time I coughed. On top of everything else, I kept passing out. This sinus infection had come on so quickly, so devastatingly. Except for a prebaby kidney infection, I had never in my life felt so awful, been so feeble. And though I had left an urgent message at my husband's Chicago office, I knew that even if he'd started for home the very instant he'd received it, it would take him nearly two hours to reach us here in the suburbs. At the rate I was fading, I feared I wouldn't last that long. Still, my main concern was for my son. Naturally, at his tender age, he had a healthy curiosity and a high activity level. He didn't understand that Mommy was too ill to keep him out of harm's way.

The television's babysitting services seemed to be working well for Nathaniel. Eventually, however, the cat seemed to have gotten bored. While I lay trembling under the blanket, Oz began flicking my earlobe and pawing at my face. His intense meowing was really getting on my nerves.

"Shut up, you stupid cat!" I growled groggily. "Can't you see I'm dying?"

Apparently, he couldn't, because Ozzie continued to relentlessly scratch at my inert form, making all kinds of loud cat noises into my overly sensitive but clogged ears. Finally, in desperation, I bolted up from my hand-crocheted cave ready to boot the cat all the way back to the Humane Society from whence he came.

However, before I could lash out at him, Ozzie scampered across the room to where my son's toy box was stashed inside the closet. Even in my blurry-eyed, cotton-headed state, I could see that Oz was trying to comfort my frightened little boy while attempting to get my attention. It took a moment for my eyes to focus—Nathaniel had somehow managed to get completely stuck inside his toy box, trapped by an avalanche of cars and his Little People Garage. My son was truly distressed and crying. When I tried to stand, the room began to sway and I nearly toppled over. Landing on my hands and knees, I fought to stay conscious.

"It's okay, Nathaniel," I called, using all of my strength and a good deal of adrenaline to creep toward him. All the while Ozzie paced back and forth in front of the toy box, gently mewing. He'd flip his long furry tail into the box, caressing Nathaniel's flushed cheek in comfort.

As soon as I reached the scene, grappled with the fallen toys, and pulled Nathaniel to safety, Ozzie, purring like a locomotive, leaned in close to my son, sniffing him all over. Satisfied that the boy was okay, the cat leaped back onto the television and began cleaning his fur. Now that all was well, Ozzie and I exchanged glances. "Thanks, cat," I offered sincerely. "I owe you one." Ozzie gave me that superior look that cats like to give fools and then merely resumed his grooming.

With my last ounce of energy, I corralled Nathaniel with his many cars and garage on the floor near my bed. Again, I promptly passed out. I must have become delusional as well, because the next time I came to, I was huddled on my side. In a dream-like trance, I thought I heard my mother's far-off voice warning, "Danger! Danger! That cat's sucking your breath away!" I figured it must be real—I could feel fur on my nose and a warm kitty body near my mouth. Opening my eyes, I realized that part was true. Ozzie's furry back was just inches from my mouth and face. His paw was stretched around my head and his slightly twitching black tail was curved over my chest. I rolled backward, sure I was being choked to death by that monstrous feline.

Seeing I was awake, Nathaniel cried cheerfully, "Ozzie play!"

Despite a sudden bout of brain-jarring coughing, I flipped onto my stomach. To my surprise, instead of having tried to suffocate me, Oz was indeed playing with Nathaniel. In an attempt to protect me from flying cars, the poor animal had turned himself into a retaining wall, molding his torso around my face, head, and throat so that the small metal cars Nathaniel aimed at me would bounce along the cat's body. Though Ozzie's expression was far less than happy, he'd nonetheless stationed himself between me and the danger zone.

"Looks like I owe you two, Oz." I reached out to stroke Ozzie's head, but he had already raced off to his roost on the television, determined to clean the nasty toy gunk from his immaculate coat.

This time I was able to stay alert long enough to interest Nathaniel in *Sesame Street* before I keeled over once more. With luck, by the time the educational program was over, Art would be home. I crossed my fingers . . . and blacked out.

When a frenzied paw smacked my face, hard and strong, and Ozzie's near howl assaulted my ears, I wasted no time on silly cat-fearing notions. I struggled to clear my brain, then followed Ozzie's genuinely frightened gaze. My son sat silent and secretive next to the electrical outlet. The unplugged lamp cord was draped over Nathaniel's leg, and he held a metal paper clip in his right hand. Concentrating as only a toddler who knows he's doing something wrong can, Nathaniel was about to stick the metal clip into the wall socket. Suddenly, Ozzie abandoned his attempts to roust me and leaped, hissing frantically, to the arm of the sofa.

"Nathaniel!" I screamed, as my head exploded and my throat bled. "No! No!"

As if to help me make my point, Ozzie rapidly swatted Nathaniel's head with his curled paw. Frightened by the sound of my voice and by Ozzie's disciplinary assault, my son jumped, dropping the paper clip harmlessly onto the floor. Scuttling over on all fours, I retrieved the clip and replugged the lamp. As I hugged Nathaniel and explained the dangers of his actions, I smiled at Ozzie. But he was already on the TV, smoothing his ruffled fur.

Moments later, Art walked through the front door. Nathaniel ran happily to his dad, and I collapsed again while babbling about antibiotics and hero cats. Satisfied that a competent babysitter had arrived, Ozzie gave a relieved sigh and slinked out of sight, no doubt anxious to give himself a thorough cleaning after all that.

I'll never understand how Ozzie sensed that he had to protect Nathaniel from those living room perils on that awful day. I shudder to think what could have happened if he hadn't been there to do it, and I am infinitely grateful that he did. So, after a doctor's visit and plenty of medicated bed rest, I recovered enough to make a trip to the local pet shop. Armed with a toy mouse stuffed with catnip, I stroked Ozzie's chest and gave him a proper thank you for his services.

"Welcome to the family, buddy. I'll never doubt your intentions again!"

Ozzie purred, bumped my chin, and then gave that mouse a meticulous tongue bath!

—*Loy Michael Cerf*

Ranch Kitties

I live on a ranch in southwest Colorado. Our place is not ideal for kitties, so it's best if a person does not get attached, that person being me. My husband likes to have cats for the practical reason of keeping down the mice population. I do, too, but my daughter and I would get so attached to the cute little fur balls. We were devastated time and again as, one by one, our little kitties disappeared. One of our cow dogs would kill them if she could catch them. We lived close to the dirt road, and they would get run over. Coyotes frequented our property, and I could only guess that is what happened to others.

Finally, we had a cat named Pretty who had longevity. We didn't get too attached to her because she was an outdoor cat and so very cautious. She was a great mouser and good company during gardening season. However, we had to make a move to another home close by. I wasn't sure if she would come with us or stay in her familiar shed.

After we moved, it was obvious our mouser was content where she was in her old home. I decided I would get a couple of kitties to be mousers at our new place. I didn't want to get attached, so they had to be outdoor kitties. I wasn't going to pet them very much, because I wanted them to be a little shy of people. They would stay in the woodshed. And when they disappeared, I wouldn't be devastated, because I would not be attached.

I brought the cute little fur balls home. I wanted females. My second cousin said, "Yep, this one is a girl and this one is a girl." When it was time to get them spayed, the vet said one had to be neutered. The female was short-haired and black with a couple of small white spots. The male tabby was long-haired with brown and gray stripes.

After a few days with my new kitties and my prevention plan in place, all was well. I barely knew the kitties were there. They hid from me when I fed them, and they were very worried about our new cow dog, Boots. (Our kitty murderer was no longer with us.) However, there was one factor I did not consider in my plan. She was about three feet tall and twenty-five pounds, with blond hair and green eyes: my granddaughter Sky.

She found out that Grandma had kitties. Sky is the true "kitten whisperer." It took her one day to have those kitties coaxed out of the woodshed, purring, and sharing her sandwich. She packed those kitties everywhere and hugged and loved them. She brought them to the porch, and Grandpa joined in. They played with the kitties together almost every day.

I would go out to feed the kitties; of course, they were on the porch. I took them to the woodshed and fed them there, because if they were on the porch, I would get attached. They purred and rubbed around my legs. I pet them only a little bit, because they liked it. I picked them up and talked to them, but not too much.

I was worried about Boots. He always acted funny around the kitties. He would stare at them and move ever so slowly close to them. The kitties got to where they half ignored it. I would scold the dog to quit staring at the kitties and go lie down.

One day the kitties were playing in the bushes and Boots gently reached through the bushes and pulled them out. My husband said, "Come look at this!" That cow dog didn't want them going behind things, and he tried to herd them here and there. It finally got to where the kitties slept with him in the doghouse.

Well, my kitties weren't half wild. They didn't stay in the woodshed, even though I still fed them there. They were so spoiled, I didn't even know if they would be good mousers. And they weren't afraid of our cow dog. Maybe they thought they were dogs. They ate with the dog. They followed my husband everywhere right along with the dog. But one thing I knew. I was not attached.

I came home from work later than usual one night. The kitties weren't on the porch like they normally were. I thought they must be doing kitty things about this time and went in to bed. The next morning I got up later than my husband, who was already out doing chores. I stepped out to the porch, but there were no kitties. Maybe they were with him. My husband finally came in, and I asked him about the kitties. He hadn't seen them since yesterday afternoon when they'd walked with him and the dog to the pond.

"To the pond!" I yelled. They had never gone that far before.

I immediately changed my clothes and headed for the pond. I called, "Here kitty, kitty," over and over again. How could my husband be so careless? There were eagles, coyotes, and other dogs out in the field. I called and called while at the pond. I looked in all directions. I knew they were lost, if not already dead. I felt so terrible. Those were my kitties. I hauled them into the vet to be fixed. I fed them. I protected them from dogs. I saved them when the grandkids got too rough. I . . . I . . . I was attached! I loved those little kitties, and now they were gone. I was devastated. I was so angry at myself because I'd gotten attached. "It's just not worth it, because kitties don't live long on a ranch with our circumstances," I said aloud.

I slowly moped my way back to the house. I was going to give my husband what-for when I saw him. I checked the ditch on my way back, just in case—no kitties. I entered the yard heavy-hearted, not knowing what might have happened to them. As I rounded the corner of the house, aching and on the verge of tears, I glanced at movement toward the doghouse. I hadn't thought to look in the doghouse. Out came Stripe, the tabby kitty, and Sally Anna, the black kitty. I stopped in my tracks and just stared for a few seconds. Then this tremendous relief and overwhelming joy came over me. They were here and okay! I picked them up and loved them. They, too, were overjoyed by the attention—and wondering why the sudden flood of affection from someone who was not attached.

Well, we still have those kitties, now cats. They are excellent mousers. Sally Anna also keeps the bunny population down. I forgave my husband, and, yes, I am very attached to Stripe and Sally Anna. They are a part of our family.

—Diana Schmitt

The Whole Kitten Caboodle

"Meee! Meee! Meee!"

A tiny kitten crawled out from between the weeds in the empty lot opposite my house. The kitten was only about six inches long, from nose to rear, and its head was the size of a Ping-Pong ball. I picked it up and looked under the tail. Female. She had bright blue eyes rimmed with thick eyelids that had only recently parted, indicating she was only a week to ten days old. And she was filthy. Clearly, the mother was no longer around. I'd seen a feral cat hanging around the vacant lot, but now that I thought about it, I hadn't seen it for several days.

Although I didn't think the kitten had a chance, I couldn't bear to leave her. So I took her home and tried to clean her up with a damp cloth. After an hour I gave up and bathed her instead. At least it drowned most of the fleas. Underneath the dirt, she was marmalade.

Then I washed out an old eyedropper and fed her with the only milk I had: UHT cow's milk (treated with ultrahigh temperatures so that it can be stored without refrigeration for several months), which even I knew was wildly unsuitable. She purred as she gulped it down and then promptly fell fast asleep in the palm of my hand. Something as small as a kitten's tail crept around my heart and clung on.

What could I do? This tiny soul was depending on me, and I hadn't a clue how to mother a kitten. Besides, she presumably needed at least four feeds a day, and I had to go to work on Monday. Since I'd let myself in for the whole kit and caboodle, I called her Kitten Caboodle.

I phoned my friend, Cecilia, who lived two hours' drive away in the countryside. Cecilia had a large family of adopted cats and dogs, so I figured she'd know more about it than I. "I've found a tiny orphaned kitten, far too young to be away from her mother. Do you know anyone who'd look after her?"

Cecilia sighed. "Oh, all right. Bring her here."

That was better than I'd hoped for.

I drove over. One of Cecilia's dogs had recently given birth. Tassat was mostly Dachshund and we had no idea about the father, but the puppies were only about twice Caboodle's size and age. Cecilia promptly put her in with them for warmth and companionship. Then she laid a major guilt trip on Tassat.

"You see this poor starving kitten? What she needs now is lovely warm milk. You remember how good that felt with your own mother, don't you? When you were pregnant and starving, we took you in and saved you. Well, now it's your turn to help."

It worked. Caboodle grew up on dog milk. It looked weird, six dark brown puppies and one marmalade kitten, all sucking away together, but they all seemed thoroughly happy with the arrangement.

Puppies grow faster than kittens. Caboodle had one bad week when her larger foster siblings' play was too boisterous for her to cope with. Then she made two important discoveries: Kittens can climb where puppies can't follow. And kittens have claws. The rest of the litter soon learned not to push her too far.

Eventually, they were weaned. Twice a day Cecilia would fill a large bowl with food for her family of rescued animals, and they'd all gather around the edge. Not Caboodle. She climbed on top of the heap and ate the patch directly underneath herself until her belly stuck out like a seahorse's. When the German shepherd gave her a friendly sniff, out came the claws and she walloped him across the nose. She'd almost starved once, and nobody was going to threaten her food supply again—even if they happened to be big enough to swallow her in two gulps. Fortunately, the dog was a big softie and didn't argue the point.

Even fully grown, Caboodle was small for a cat—physically, that is. We used to wonder how she managed to fit so much personality into such a petite body. The dogs enjoyed chasing the cats up trees. They hadn't the slightest intention of hurting them; they just liked to make sure they got plenty of nice healthy exercise. But when they rushed at Caboodle, barking like crazy, she gave them a disdainful stare—as if to say, *You and whose army?*—and continued walking at exactly the same pace as she had been, while the dogs stood around looking embarrassed.

For all that, she was very affectionate, especially with her foster brothers and sisters. She was particularly fond of washing their faces for them. In fact, she'd hold them down by their floppy ears to prevent them from wandering away in the middle of a wash.

In time, she had her first litter of kittens. Since she couldn't possibly have remembered her own mother, I worried she wouldn't know where to start. But she was brilliant. She kept her family in the bottom of the wardrobe and left them only for meals. I think her canine brothers and sisters were rather relieved that she was too busy washing her children to bother her siblings.

It was a good time for an undersized cat and her kittens to stay indoors. A neighbor's Graafian hunting dog kept "visiting" and stealing anything edible.

It was a huge beast, almost the size of a donkey, and even Cecilia's German shepherd was terrified of it.

At last the great day came when the kittens ventured outdoors for the first time. Caboodle sat in the kitchen doorway, with one eye on her offspring and the other on Cecilia, who was cooking lunch. Well, it was bound to happen, and next thing you know, the huge dog lumbered along the path to the front door. And then it sniffed a kitten.

A bolt of marmalade lightning shot out the door and zoomed up the bank beside the path. From there, Caboodle leaped onto the dog's back and dug in all eighteen claws, hard. The dog hurtled up the garden path, howling, with Caboodle riding on its back like a jockey. *Ow! Ow! Ow! Ow! Ow! Ow!* . . . and the howls faded off into the distance.

Meanwhile, Cecilia didn't know which sort of hysterics to have. It was like a trailer for the world's best comedy film, but she had little hope of ever seeing Caboodle again.

Forty minutes later, Caboodle strolled home, looking as nonchalant as—well, there's really nothing as nonchalant as a cat, is there?

Whenever I feel I'm too small to tackle a problem, I remember Caboodle.

—*Sheila Crosby*

Cat's Choice

I backed through the old screen door, a large bucket of soapy water in hand, and turned to dump the dirty water over the deck railing. I had just cleaned the paintbrush I was using to brighten some wood trim in the eighty-year-old cottage my husband and I had recently purchased. *That's the next repair to this house,* I mused as I passed through the door and back into the kitchen. The handle required a sincere yank to close; otherwise, the door stood ajar about an inch. *I'll remind Bill tonight.*

Bill, my husband, was working the Saturday night shift of his second job. It was close to midnight, and I scurried to complete my tasks before he returned home, so we could have a few moments of together time before evening's end.

As I laid the wet paintbrush on newspaper to dry, I heard the metallic *ka-chunk* of the old door. I dried my hands and gave the door a proper closing. When I turned toward the living room archway, I spied just the tip of a furry orange tail. I shook my head. *Did a cat get in through the door, or am I seeing things?* I wondered if I had perhaps sniffed a little too much paint that evening. Moving toward the living room to investigate further, I spotted a fat, fluffy orange tabby with a pink nose the color of bubble gum lying on his side, claiming the living room as his own. He was identical in appearance to my childhood pet, Kiki.

Still not totally convinced this was nothing more than a paint-induced hallucination, I got down on all fours and crawled toward him. He started to purr with the rhythm of a small motor and rolled on his back, inviting me to rub his flabby tummy. I complied, gingerly at first, and the vibration of his purr reached a delighted crescendo. In a moment of spontaneous abandon, I kissed his soft belly. His fur smelled of moist earth and pine needles, and I inhaled deeply before lifting my head. Bill walked through the front door at just that moment.

"What's this?" he asked as he stood over the two of us.

"I'm not sure. He just snuck in through the kitchen door."

"Well, sneak him back out."

"Huh? I thought you like cats."

"Not that one." Bill pointed toward the tabby with more than a hint of disapproval. "He's so big and"—Bill grappled for the proper adjective—"and orange."

We were both too tired to argue, so I lifted the dead weight of the slack cat and placed him on the deck outside. That's where he remained until I opened the kitchen door early the next morning.

I invited the tabby in and reached into my pantry cabinet for the only cat-friendly food I could find, a can of tuna.

"I smell tuna," Bill remarked as he shuffled into the kitchen wearing his robe and pajamas. He opened his eyes a little wider. "Not that cat again!"

"He decided he likes it here, and I'm not going to argue with him." I turned toward Bill with a scowl of resolve. "And you're not going to argue with him about it either."

From that day forward, Moo, as the tabby came to be known, never left the confines of the cottage or its yard. It wasn't long before he started to watch evening television with us, curled on Bill's lap. Soon after that, he joined us in our king-sized bed, sleeping snugly against the footboard. Moo became an important part of our family, sharing in our happiness and comforting us in our sorrows in the soft, warm way only a cat can.

Nearing the time of Moo's second anniversary of adopting us, my aging mother suffered a serious accident. Her leg had been badly cut, and she remained in the hospital for months while doctors fought a life-threatening skin infection that had set in. Eventually, victory over the infection was won, but complications from diabetes stopped the wound from healing properly for a long time. Walking was difficult for her, and she required my help daily. The responsibilities of a job, caring for her and my father, who suffered from a plethora of his own health issues, in addition to my own household chores wore on me heavily. I looked forward to the bright moment each evening when I returned home to be greeted by my waiting Moo. I could tell him all my troubles, and he always comforted me with a dependable purr and a sympathetic look in his golden eyes.

However, the stress of my family situation eventually sent me to my own sickbed. After several days of recuperation, Moo jumped into bed with me and lay across my aching belly. Within a few minutes I had the sensation of the pain and discomfort of my ailment leaving my body, as if it were somehow transferring to Moo through osmosis. I left my sickbed well that afternoon.

Shortly after, my mother was pronounced fully recovered by her doctor. I returned home that day full of joy. "Moo, everything is all better now," I eagerly told him. He looked at me with his soulful eyes, and I said a silent prayer of gratitude for the good news and for Moo, too. I opened the old kitchen door and let him out into the yard.

That was the last time I ever saw Moo.

"We just have to get another cat," my husband said as he rubbed my back while it heaved with sobs.

I was heartbroken. A month had passed since I had last seen Moo, and just the thought of him set me to tears. "I don't know if we'll ever find another cat like Moo," I said.

"No two cats are ever the same. Maybe we'll find an even better one."

"I doubt it," I countered, rising from the kitchen chair. I paused a moment, noting the almost pleading look in Bill's eyes. "All right, let's go to the shelter next Friday . . . just to look."

Friday came, and we made the short drive to the local animal shelter. Margie, the adoption coordinator, opened the door to the cattery. I scanned the periphery for any sign of a fat, orange tabby. Not one in sight. I walked ahead, still hoping to find a suitable replacement for Moo. As I turned back, I saw a small black cat following close behind Bill. "Look behind you," I pointed.

Bill hovered over the small black cat with two evenly matched white front paws and crooned, "You look just like my first cat, Bootsy."

Margie remarked that the black cat, Charley, was a sweet little boy who needed a quiet home, adding that his owner had abandoned him at the shelter a month before. His paperwork revealed that he was returned to the shelter within a week of Moo's final day with us. The decision was clear: Charley would be coming home with us.

As we walked out of the cattery toward the parking lot with Charley tucked safely inside a carrier, a shelter volunteer who was walking a dog called out, "Which one did you take?"

Bill called back, "Charley. He chose us."

"That's how it is with cats," she laughed. "You have to let them choose you."

Yes, that is how it is with cats.

—*Monica A. Andermann*

Why My Cat May Someday Cost Me My Marriage

The cat smells bad. She no longer has the sweet, soft, fresh smell of well-groomed kitty fur. Now she smells like ammonia—or, in layman's terms, pee.

"Are you cleaning the litter box?" I ask my husband. "Daily?"

"Why am I always the one who gets blamed?" he asks. "Why am I responsible for the cat smelling like pee?"

"Maybe she's sick," I say. "Let's keep an eye on her."

Worried, I hop on line and enter my query:

CATS SMELL URINE

Five million sites on how to remove the smell of cat urine from carpets, furniture, suitcases, and clothing fill the screen.

I try again:

CATS SMELL FUR AMMONIA
CATS STINK URINE DISEASE
CATS SMELLY PEE DISEASE

Nothing, although I now know fifty different ways to remove urine stains from cashmere. I give it one last try:

CATS ICKY YUCK SMELL PROBABLY CAUSED BY HUSBANDS NON-SANITARY METHODS FOR FECES AND URINE CLUMP DISPOSAL

Bingo! A site for Feline Lower Urinary Tract Disease (FLUTD) appears. FLUTD, I read, takes on many different forms and stages. The most serious is when tiny crystals appear in a cat's urine. Death is possible.

I race downstairs. My husband is watching TV.

"Have you seen any signs of crystals?" I shriek.

"Huh?" he says.

"Fluted! Fatal cat disease! Crystals in the urine! Have you seen any?"

I race back upstairs, not giving him a chance to answer. The Web site indicates cats with urinary tract infections need to drink a lot of water, adding that with their inquisitive nature, cats are more likely to drink out of bowls placed in odd spots around the home. They also say some cats enjoy drinking from running water.

The next afternoon my husband approaches me. "Why is my shower running?" he asks.

"In case the cat gets thirsty," I reply.

Later he appears again, clenching a dripping sock in one hand. "Did you know there's a pan of water at the top of the stairs?"

"Yes," I say. "There are also bowls of water under the dining room table, in the laundry room, on top of the dresser in the guest bedroom, and under the bathroom sink."

"Why don't you just take her to the vet?" he begs.

I take her the next day. Returning home, I release the cat and stand in front of my husband.

"Well?"

"It's not good," I begin.

He puts a hand to his heart. "Oh, no. You mean she's . . . she's . . . "

"Relax, the cat is fine," I say, waving away his concern. "We're the ones in trouble." I pause, wondering how to break the news, and decide the direct route is best. "We have to wipe her butt. Daily."

He blinks. Opens his mouth to say something. Thinks better of it. Opens it again.

"Why?" finally comes out.

"Because," I sigh. "She's too fat, and her skin is folding over and trapping pieces of … you know . . . in the area of her—"

"Lalalalala," says my husband, sticking fingers in both ears. "I can't hear you. Lalalalala . . ."

I give him a look that suggests he find a different means to express himself.

He removes his fingers. "Look here," he says. "You told me cats were easy. You promised all we had to do was feed and water and occasionally pet them. And *now* you're telling me we have to catch and hold down a creature—with claws—so we can wash poo from between the fatty folds of its butt?"

"Um, actually," I say with a meek smile, "you have to wipe her butt. Poo makes me sick."

After several rounds of negotiations and the threat of divorce, I agree to at least hold the cat while he wipes.

I lull the cat into a false sense of security by combing her for twenty minutes. When she is relaxed and purring, I motion for my husband, hiding low at the top of the stairs with a wet towel, to approach.

"Is the towel the right temperature?" I whisper. He glares at me.

"Right," I say. "I'm sure it's fine."

Gingerly, as if afraid she is wired with explosives, he lifts the cat's tail. Her ears perk, and she twists her head to look at him.

"Easy now," he says, wiping.

Mrow, says the cat.

"I think she likes it," I encourage him.

"That thought terrifies me," says my husband, prying open folds of fat to clean between them.

Rrrrrrrr. The sound coming from her was half growl, half purr.

"Hurry up," I urge.

"Do you want this end of the job?" he asks. We finish cleaning, and my husband attempts to hand me the brown-stained cloth.

I make gagging noises and wave him away. "I can't even look at that."

"Well, what should I do with it?"

"Washing machine."

"Ewwww, gross! I'm not putting kitty poo in the washing machine."

I look at him. "Please remind me to never bear you children," I say.

I make an already bad situation worse by telling my mom about our newly acquired need for feline butt wiping. She is full of suggestions.

"Maybe you need a bigger litter box. Maybe she just can't maneuver properly."

"The litter box is fine. She is just too fat."

"Well, I've never heard of such a thing. Everyone knows cats clean themselves."

"Mom, the vet said—"

"The vet! What makes him such an expert?"

"Twelve years of schooling?" I say.

I've stopped telling people we have to wipe the cat's butt. My friends with kids laugh at me. My friends without pets think I'm nuts. My friends with pets, especially cat owners, say nothing but look infuriatingly smug that they don't have to do the same.

So it's just me, the cat, and my husband, bearing out our dirty little secret. And now every Monday, along with taking out the trash and watering the plants, we have the added chore of washing a week's worth of poo towels. Yes, it's gross. But at least the cat smells better.

—Dena Harris

This story was published under the title "The Great Cat Butt Wiping Adventure" in Cat & Kitten *magazine, September 2005.*

Dream Cat

I hallucinated for weeks in the hospital. Pink and gray cats climbed onto the windowsills, leapt the bedrails, and settled themselves heavily on my chest.

During my months in an intensive care burn unit, my mother visited daily. She told me about the animal shelter near the medical center where she often stopped to walk the overjoyed dogs, as much for her therapy and relief as theirs. She mentioned the rows of large, mature, pouting cats peering out from behind wire mesh. Often left by infirm or deceased owners, she said you could read the bewilderment in their glaring faces. Stuck in my bed, all but motionless, I felt a kinship with those confused, scared cats down the road.

During my long recovery, the same nightmare recurred. I came upon a house with a grand wrap-around porch covered with mewing cats flicking their tails. More cats tumbled out of the rooms inside, but I held only a single can of tuna. The source of the cat dreams remained a mystery. Then a wise friend clued me in. "Those crying cats are your unmet needs."

In the dream I had two good hands, but in reality all ten fingers had been claimed by the fire. Now, securing a leash onto the dog's collar ended in wrestling matches. But my mother's dog never reacted to my scarred face; he only wanted to romp.

Once I moved out on my own, I missed the balm of animal presence. I felt abandoned by friends from my former active life and rejected by most people afraid of my looks. My face, a quilt of skin grafts, would require years of reconstruction. I was disabled. I had trouble repotting a plant. How could I manage an animal? How would I open the food cans?

At a Boston animal shelter, I found myself prowling the stacked cages. Though I feared kittens' claws on my delicate grafted skin, I hoped to find a placid older cat that had already been declawed. Yet, I am normally against this procedure that robs a cat of its essential joy and defense. Cats use paws as hands. I identified with losing that dexterity.

In the chaos of barking dogs and slamming doors, kids and couples cooed over the kittens. I rubbed a fuzzy head pressed against the bars, asleep. The gray sprawled in an unruly pose, nothing like the memory of my refined tuxedo, Gatsby. This cat was the color of lint. One paw extended upside-down in full body stretch and hooked onto my sweater.

"Anything over six months is hard to move here," said the woman refilling water dishes.

The card above the gray read: *Two years. Given up for allergies.*

After pulling me closer, the claws retracted. I had been chosen.

As I wrote out a check, the washed-out calico shrugged off her yawns and strutted on the counter, flashing her white legs and one bar of orange tiger stripes. A white bib set off her faded colors. Her green-gold eyes fixed on the loose cockatiels behind the counter, while I stared at the lavish tattoos of dogs and cats decorating the clerk's forearms.

"What will you name her?" my friend and driver Lily asked.

When we'd hit the tunnel on Storrow Drive, a crystal voice erupted from the carrier. As the volume swelled, her timbre said it all: opera. The plain-Jane gray with the high-tone voice would be Carmen.

Carmen changed my perception of cat style. The force of her diva persona rescued me with her zest and spirit. She works a room. The repertoire: the swagger, the growl at any footsteps in the hall, the staccato chatter, questions in tonal mews, trills, and the lament. When I head out the door, the drama ensues. On cue, the actress races to the center of the living room rug, pirouettes, and topples with a wail or a pitiful eek, one paw draped over her face.

I must plan ahead for helping hands for nail trims and carrier excursions. Needing cat assistance or cat-sitting helped me meet neighbors—and to convert those unfamiliar with cat grace. Pets connect people to conversations and community. Amazed at how many people asked if I carry a wallet photo of my cat, I now do.

Carmen anchors my day. At dawn, I feel the press of a paw on my face, gently hinting at the daggers beneath. From the window we watch the skyline come into color, and Carmen chirps through the screen to the pigeons that coo under the eaves. I manage to feed her, brush her with a wire curry, and scoop litter, because I must. In return, I live with a psychic roommate tuned to my every mood. Following my many surgeries, Carmen selects a bed corner and appoints herself nurse-cat sentinel.

I had sought out a calm, older cat, but Carmen remains full of zest at eight years old. All feline acrobats possess raw talent. Like the spring release of a taut rubber band, in a single fluid bound she uses the door ledge as a balance beam. She plays a jaguar, raking her six-foot scratching tree. Still, though she wraps her four legs around my arm, she never claws me. I remember visiting a man whose cat rubbed on his wheelchair each time it passed by. Cats are agile in their loyalty, recognizing and expressing love in its myriad shapes and unconventional forms.

My charismatic diva with the seemingly plain-Jane coat is, to me, as lovely as she is loyal. Call her diluted, but I prefer pastel. In sunlight and in moonlight, my cat wears the plush sheen of pussy willow. A tricolor treasure who shimmers in her pale frosty coat, Carmen adds color to my days. And every evening, she settles heavily on my chest, my serene feline dream.

—Holly Leigh

Raggedy Andy

The ringing of the phone jarred us from our relaxation. It was Vicki, president of our Humane Society. "I know it's not your week for rescue, but this one's in your neighborhood. Would you mind checking it out?"

"He may already be dead," Vicki warned. "He probably hasn't eaten in days. He's been lying on the back step of an elderly lady's house. She wants someone to come pick him up."

Arriving at the house, we were met by a decidedly nonelderly female. She explained that this was her grandmother's house and whispered, "No, the cat isn't dead, and no, he isn't starving. I've been feeding him. Grandma doesn't like cats."

We walked around to the back, and there he was, a heap of dirty, matted black fur. I gingerly picked him up and placed him in the carrier.

I called the vet, using my husband's cell phone. By then, it was nearly 10:30 P.M., and with a tired sigh, he said, "I'll meet you in fifteen minutes."

Upon arrival at the vet's office, we reluctantly laid the cat on the cold metal table. My husband stayed with him as I went to call Vicki. Since our Humane Society was supported only by donations, we had recently voted to limit expenditures on any animal to $100. I needed to keep her posted on the condition of this brave little guy, although my husband and I had already decided, without the need for discussion, that we would pay any fees over what the Humane Society would approve. The cat ensured his good fortune when he hopped over to my husband using only his back legs, looking like a mutant kangaroo. As he snuggled into my husband's chest, all we could think was, *How can you put a dollar amount on helping an animal with that much gumption and affection?*

The vet explained that the cat had broken front paws, which had been healing incorrectly for at least two weeks, one so crookedly it looked as if it would require amputation. He asked if we had considered euthanasia, since the cat's care would require a considerable amount over the $100, and "he might end up with only three legs." My husband's only question, bless his heart, was "Will he be able to get around on three legs?"

"Oh, sure," the vet said.

"Then there's no question. Let's try to make him better."

Andy, as we called him, stayed in the hospital for two days and came home with a bandaged paw. Over the next few days, the pungent smell from that area made it abundantly clear that something wasn't right. Back we went, days ahead of his scheduled checkup, only to find that infection had set in. The smell was rotting flesh. This time he stayed for three weeks while the doctor bandaged, cleaned, and ran warm water over his paw every day. We visited daily, until the vet gently explained that Andy got more upset when we left after each visit than he would if we just came back when he was well enough to go home. "We're taking good care of him, I promise," he said. We grudgingly agreed to end our daily visits, but called frequently to make sure Andy got the attention he deserved.

Nearly a month after we had found him in a heap, we brought Andy home again—with all four legs. We had a dog and three cats of our own, and we knew it wouldn't be wise to try to keep him in the house while he was healing, so we boarded up our screened-in porch. Not as simple as it sounds, the process included measuring, having plywood cut, painting (so it looked good on the outside too), and screwing the individual panels to the frame. Weather stripping was applied, and since we didn't want the porch to be too dark, an $80 sheet of acrylic replaced one of the plywood panels so that Andy could enjoy the sunshine during his forced sabbatical. (The neighbors asked what in the world we were doing. When we explained we were building a "cat house," they got strangely quiet. Surely they didn't think we meant *that* kind of cat house!)

As the nights progressed from just chilly to downright cold, I was sure the porch wouldn't be warm enough. We proceeded to build another shelter inside the cat house on the porch, with walls made of wooden boxes, layers of blankets on the floor, and even a roof. The chimney was our crowning achievement. Since the porch was unheated, we ran some flexible hose from a heat duct inside the house and through the window into the porch. Not only that, but we also put a ceramic heater in the room, and turned it on for a few minutes to take the chill out of the air before we went to bed each evening.

Andy seemed comfortable with his sleeping quarters and had frequent supervised visits inside our house. He seemed to be recovering quite well, but then I noticed a substance on his hindquarters. We took him back to the doctor, where we discovered a hole in the thigh of his hind leg, likely from a BB shot. The partially healed wound had probably reopened because of Andy's improved mobility.

As our interaction with Andy increased, we also noticed a bald spot on his neck. Considering he is the only cat we've ever known who has run in fear of a dangling length of brightly colored yarn, we can only surmise that someone must have tried to hang him. Most cats have never met a string they didn't like; Andy never met a string he did like. He also had an inordinate fear of tennis shoes.

We spent many hours trying to earn the trust of this stunning creature. Sometimes I would sit quietly beside him, holding my breath, hoping he would crawl into my lap. He would often repay my kindness with his purr, which was akin to the sound of an outboard motor and nearly as loud. Sometimes we would try to help him exercise by playing hide and seek with our hands behind a soft blanket. Although we were very busy at the time we met Andy, our priorities shifted almost unnoticeably once he came into our lives.

So where is Andy today? I would love to tell you we were able to keep him, but we knew ours was not the best home for this special creature that was always beautiful on the inside and was now beautiful to look at as well. Six months after we met Andy, the Humane Society called to say they thought they had found him a home. I was heartbroken. He was nearly completely healed, and I had been secretly plotting how we might blend him into our family.

Sometimes what our hearts want is not necessarily the best thing for the animals in our care.

Andy's potential new mom, Elaine, came to meet him on a weekend. It was love at first sight. When I heard that her husband's name was Andrew and their daughter's name was Andrea, I knew Andy was going to the perfect home.

I cried when she picked him up to take him away, but I kept telling myself it was the best thing for Andy. I cried again a week later when I found a beautiful Easter lily sitting on my front porch. The card attached was from Andy's new family, thanking us for allowing Andy to join them. How fitting to receive a flower symbolizing new beginnings to celebrate Andy's new beginning. This time, my tears came from joy.

A few weeks later, an envelope arrived with several pictures showing a much-loved Andy, with his gorgeously sleek black coat and spellbinding golden eyes. The most telling photo, though, shows him seated regally in a lovely, and expensive, handmade basket. Andy was definitely home.

That's why we do what we do. We find them, rescue them, heal them, and love them. Then we give them up, so that when we find another feline in need of assistance, we can rescue, heal, and love again.

—Linda Bruno

Papa and Misha

I don't know why I called my stepfather "Papa." It was probably because that's what my daughter started calling him as a child and the name stuck. Before, I'd always called him Stanley, the Americanized version of his Lithuanian name, Stanislaus.

When my sister and I were eleven, Stanley married our mother. He was renowned for his skill in using a boning knife in the meat-packing plants that had made Sioux City, Iowa, a thriving town. We saw our stepfather as a strict, hard man. Certainly, we never imagined he'd be the sort who would love and care for a tiny cat.

Long after my daughter, my husband, and I left Iowa, a neighbor approached my mother and Papa. She had a litter of kittens to get rid of. Somehow, a child had gotten hold of one and squeezed its neck so hard that the poor thing couldn't make a sound.

The mute kitty was the runt of the litter. No one would take a puny kitten who couldn't even purr. The woman didn't want to kill the little thing, and wondered if Mama and Papa would consider giving her a home.

"No," my mother said at the same time Papa said, "Sure."

Misha went home with Papa, starting a love affair that extended into old age.

I first saw them together when my daughter and I visited during a summer vacation. Misha, even at five or six years, was scarcely larger than Papa's huge hand. A tabby with beautiful coloring, she had hazel eyes rimmed with gold and medium-length hair. Small as she was, she had a fierce temperament and a mind of her own—both of which she displayed often, to everyone except Papa. The big, gray-haired man and the tiny, silent cat understood each other. They spoke a language that needed no sounds.

To anyone who entered the house, there was never a question whose cat she was. She gave my mother the cold shoulder, a feeling my mother returned. Even with Papa, Misha wasn't the most demonstrably loving cat. He built a house for her in the yard under the front living room window, and she was happy spending her time there. She ate outside and played outside and demanded little in the way of human attention. By then, Papa had given up the packing houses to build and manage two apartment buildings in town. Each morning he'd leave for work, stopping first to feed and greet Misha.

"Good morning, Mishila," he'd say, scratching behind her ears. She'd twist and wind around his legs, rubbing against him, craning into his fingers. He'd give her breakfast, she'd wave her tail good-bye, and he'd go off to work.

Misha rarely ventured inside. Only when winter snow covered the door to her little house did she reluctantly enter the big house—and then spent most of her time on the bedside table where she could see outside. When the snow abated, she turned up her nose as well as her tail at any invitation or coaxing to remain indoors.

The big house sat on a steep lot. The front was street level, with a basement apartment located down a flight of sixteen concrete steps beside the house. From there, the yard dropped away on a sharp grade for another hundred yards or so. Near the bottom of the hill, an apple tree needed to be trimmed, and one spring day Papa set off to do the job.

The afternoon air was still and hot. Papa walked outside and spoke to Misha with his usual mix of Lithuanian-English. He dropped a spot of leftover lunch— what he called a "slobovian" meal, a blend of leftover vegetables and meat mixed with ketchup—into her bowl. "I see you later, Mishila," he murmured, stroking her back. She preened under his attention, looked up with big eyes, and licked her chops. Then, as usual, she turned back to her own world.

Papa retrieved a saw from the back of his truck and hefted a ladder onto his shoulder. Jostling the ladder into a comfortable position, he headed for the backyard. The row of bushes hiding the neighbor's yard was full of white, bridal wreath flowers, and roses bloomed on the strip of land leading to the stairs. Roses and peonies formed islands of color and scent in the backyard near the clotheslines.

He ignored the bees flitting from bloom to bloom as well as the nodding heads of pansies and petunias along the back of the house. In his mind, he'd already climbed the tree and planned how to trim the dead branches and where to stack the brush. He was used to working alone, even when the job involved danger. It never would have occurred to him that no one was home or that the tree would be hidden from street view. He gave no credence to the opinion that a man who'd reached his sixties had no business climbing trees or easing out onto limbs weakened by age and weather. Call a professional? What for? This—taking care of his own place, his own business—is what he did, what he'd always done.

It was quiet at the bottom of the hill. A thick stand of lilacs along with a variety of other bushes and trees blocked noise from the next street down, and the road on which Mama and Papa's house sat, was too far off for noise. The ladder made a *thunk* when Papa dropped the top against the solid trunk of the apple. He pulled the ladder's feet away from the base of the tree and then shook it to make sure it was steady and firm. He looked up through the branches to the sun far overhead, barely discernable through the limbs, thick with leaves. He spotted the first area of deadwood about ten feet up. Focused only on the knowledge that the work had to be done, he grabbed the saw handle and climbed up.

How long had he been at it, an hour? Two? He swept his arm across his forehead, letting his shirt-sleeve soak up the sweat that had beaded his face and run into his eyes. Since starting work, he'd scrambled another five or six feet higher. Heat spiraled up through the branches. Papa's breath came heavy. He sat back and examined the amount of work left. Wiping his brow again, he decided to keep at it a little longer and then stop, finished or not.

Scooting out, he expertly gripped the limb with his knees. He sawed, then leaned back to kick the wood off the branch and to the ground. Sweat dripped into his eyes. Heat swamped him. Before he knew what was happening, he slipped. He tried to release the saw, but couldn't seem to let go. His free hand sought purchase on the bark, but the branch was too thick. His leg hit a limb; his arm scraped another, knocking the saw from his hand. He fell nearly sixteen feet, landing on his right leg and then hitting the ground hard with his arm and head. Mercifully, he blacked out.

When he opened his lids, soft hazel eyes peered into his. Why Misha had come to find him or how she knew to, he didn't know. She nudged his forehead with her nose and licked his face. He took a breath and then took stock.

Shifting his right leg sent waves of pain roiling through him. Spots danced before his eyes. Misha patted his cheek with her paws and stared at him with intent. He fought nausea. Not only were his leg, foot, and ankle useless, he'd also rolled farther down the hill when he fell and had no way to get to help except to crawl his way up to the house.

He pulled himself a few feet. Tears competed with the sweat pouring down his face before he passed out again.

When he woke, the sun beat down on his back and Misha's raspy little tongue was bathing his face. She bent her head and nudged his forehead. With superhuman strength stemming from the knowledge that he wouldn't be found for hours unless he moved, Papa clawed several yards uphill before giving up consciousness. Once again, when he came to, Misha was there, licking the sweat from his face and imparting her own brand of silent encouragement. Wake up. Move. Climb.

Several times more, Papa crawled and passed out on his slow ascent to the house. Each time, the little cat was there, letting him know he wasn't alone. The tiny, quiet animal kept him going. Up the hill, up the steep flight of concrete steps, along the sidewalk, and up more steps into the house, Misha never left his side.

For some reason, Papa called my mother at work instead of an ambulance. She couldn't drive, so her boss brought her to the house, where they found a ferocious Misha sitting on an unconscious Papa's chest. The little cat turned tiger, bristling, arching her back, and swiping, claws out, ready to fight anyone or anything who might harm the vulnerable man. Only when she was convinced they were there to help did she relinquish her defensive position.

Though not as devastating as they could have been, Papa's injuries were extensive—a concussion and five broken bones in his right leg, foot, and ankle. He'd worsened the damage greatly by dragging himself up the hill and into the house, but again, not as much as he could have. Regardless, Papa was convinced he would have died lying under the big apple tree at the bottom of the hill had it not been for Misha.

A few years later, when Papa wasn't nearly old enough but when Misha was long past her prime, he died unexpectedly. The night after his burial, a clear June evening, Misha tapped at the front door and sat patiently. I let her in. She wandered from room to room. I lifted her onto Papa's bed, which she explored for a while, and then she went to the door and waited to be let out. The next morning a neighbor came to tell Mama that the cat was dead in her yard. I buried her under a peony bush under the front window of their house.

Papa rescued Misha when she was a young, damaged kitten. She returned the favor many years later by giving Papa the strength and encouragement he needed to save himself. When Papa was forced to let go of life, so did the cat he loved. Misha, the silent little tabby with the heart of a tigress, lived her life well. I think Papa did, too. Very well, indeed.

—*Anne Krist*

Hail to the Queen

The orange tabby showed up on the front porch of our Montana farmhouse in mid-October, looking quite pregnant. Because of the season and her coloring, we named her Autumn, and she quickly settled in. A few weeks and no kittens later, the vet pronounced "healthy cat, just fat."

Whatever her past life, she had obviously lived with dogs before and wasn't bothered a bit by their canine ways. Alfre, the Samoyed-retriever mix who'd come to us as an abandoned puppy with a shrunken tummy and bloody paws, formed a close bond with Autumn, and the two often napped together, the furry white dog curled around the full-figured tabby. Our two young border collies tried to herd her, but she'd hop on a chair or climb a tree and ignore them. One afternoon when one of the collies got a little bossy, Autumn swatted the dog on the nose and sent her tumbling off the front porch. After that, there was little doubt who was at the top of the animal kingdom in our house.

Years passed—years in which Autumn grew no slimmer and showed little interest in the out-of-doors. We moved from farm country to the woods at the base of the Swan Mountains in Montana, living on acres of dense pine and fir forest laced with snowberry and wild spirea, black hawthorn, birch, and aspen. Serviceberry, ceanothus, and a hundred other shrubs and forbs created a lush understory where a cat could roam for hours. But Autumn quickly established her domain—inside. She was Queen of the Fireplace, stretching out in front of the glass window and soaking up the warmth the gas flames gave off. Dame of the Davenport, her realm the middle cushion, where her short gold hairs formed the shape of a crown on the dark green upholstery. Empress of the Office, where she spent most mornings on the red willow love seat that faces my desk, raising her regal head only at unfamiliar sounds: in winter, the heavy snow sliding off the metal roof and crashing to the deck below, startling us both; in early spring, the northern flickers trying in vain to pluck insulation for their nests from the roof vents; a heavy summer rain; the grinding noise of the propane truck making its first delivery in fall.

I didn't mind Autumn's preference for the hearth and couch. Despite the lesson she'd taught the border collie on the front porch and my own love of the woods, I feared that the wild animals who lived there—coyote, badger, fox, and raccoon—would make easy pickings of my sweet, innocent cat.

I didn't know Autumn as well as I thought.

This far north, summer evenings are glorious sensory treats: the clear blue afternoon skies give way to pink-and-gold sunsets, flecked with red in bad fire years. Fresh breezes spread the butterscotch scent of pine, thick in the air on days when neighbors have been cutting wood for winter. Songbirds entertain, and the great horned owl who lives in the lodge pole forest on the southwest corner of our land hoots for hours, a bass line underscoring the rhythmic peace of the mountainside. One August evening we sat on the front deck as the light faded to black and watched the Perseid meteor showers in the northeast sky. I opened the door to head in for the night. Autumn slipped past me and headed outside. I was sure she'd be back soon, but as darkness deepened and she hadn't returned, our concern grew. My husband and I took turns calling her name; she was that rare cat who actually responds when called. But not that night. We walked around the yard calling and calling. Finally, we fell into bed, though neither of us slept.

After midnight, we heard a shriek from the woods east of the house. We both jumped up, threw on our clothes, and dashed downstairs, flash-lights in hand. We crossed the yard and headed for the woods, listening again. In the moonlight, we exchanged looks, agreeing wordlessly not to call her name; we didn't want to tempt her to respond and let a predator know where she was. So we made other noises as we searched the woods, pushing the brush and branches roughly, stepping on sticks, hoping to frighten off whatever wild creature had her in its sights. We heard more yelling, but couldn't identify the source—no wild animal cry that we recognized and certainly not a sound a cat would make.

But still no sign of Autumn. I went back to the house to get Alfre, thinking either she would sniff out the cat or the cat would make a break for free-dom when she realized the dog was on the scene. As Alfre and I crossed the yard, Autumn emerged from the woods completely unscathed. She paused to brush noses with Alfre, hopped onto the front porch, and stepped inside the house as though noth-ing unusual had happened.

That's when we realized the screech that woke us wasn't Autumn crying out in pain. It was Autumn letting her would-be stalker know who was Queen of the Woods.

Autumn lived several more years after her encounter with the Thing in the Woods, dying peacefully at seventeen. She remained content to spend most of her time indoors, but in her last few weeks, she often came outside with us, spending hours curled underneath a blue spruce behind the house or dozing at the edge of the woods. I think now that as Autumn sensed her own death approaching, she returned deliberately to a more primal place. A place where life and death often meet. A place where she'd met death herself once and sent it screaming.

Animals who have been abandoned, especially those who've been abused, as we suspect Autumn had been, are often the sweetest, so relieved to have found steady love that they give theirs freely. But Autumn taught me that they also have great reserves of strength and will and queenly courage.

—*Leslie Ann Budewitz*

Motherly Ties

At first the small gray tabby looked like any other animal abandoned on the doorstep of the Saint Charles County Humane Society. It was an unfortunate and too-frequent occurrence at the small, no-kill shelter. But this cat presented a special problem. Her swollen belly revealed rippling movement that could mean only one thing—kittens. The shelter was full, so when I arrived for my volunteer shift, Carmen, the shelter's director, asked if I'd foster the cat.

"But I don't know anything about delivering kittens."

"Cats have an instinct about these things. She'll know what to do," Carmen said as she balanced an armload of supplies. "Don't worry."

Unfortunately, if I excelled at anything, it was worry. I gritted my teeth and packed the car with an assortment of kitty necessities, leaving just enough space for the crate. As I loaded it into the car, the cat glared at me from the back corner of the enclosure, where she was crouched, taut with anxiety. Was it my imagination or did I read the word "incompetent" in those golden eyes? My anxiety escalated.

"All right, mama cat, let's go," I said cheerily, hoping to win her over with charm.

Our one-sided conversation continued as I drove the slowest and smoothest route. After all, what expectant mother wants to be jostled? I didn't know whether my passenger was impressed or not, as she maintained a sphinx-like stillness and silence the entire ride.

At home, it took three trips to move everything to the foster room. The food, fresh water, and all-important litter box were arranged in record time. Since cats like hiding places, I found a large cardboard box to use as a bed. An opening cut in front and towel draped over the top created a cozy mini-cave. I surveyed my handiwork. Though the feline birthing room had no cable or bedside phone, it looked good.

I opened the crate door. Mama cat stalked out and stretched her bulky body. Then she set off to examine the room like a queen inspecting the royal guard. Not a thing slowed her scrutiny until she reached the bed

I'd fashioned for her. With a dubious look, she sniffed it from bottom to top before climbing inside. When her front legs began to rhythmically massage the bedding, I knew I'd passed my first test.

Unlike her mother, my fourteen-year-old daughter, Jessica, had no apprehensions about the tabby. Deep in the throes of a girly adolescence, my youngest child confined her worries to the state of her social life. She couldn't have been more delighted to discover our guest was well on her way to multiplying.

"That means when the kittens come we'll be foster grandparents," she announced.

Since grandparents tend to be smart people, I waited for the wisdom of the ages to descend and provide me with some guidance. When that didn't happen, I consulted my oracle, the Internet, for advice.

Neither Jessica nor I could wait for the blessed event—she out of excitement, I out of fear. I checked the room for action a dozen times a day. Whenever the door opened, I hoped to see kittens—a done deal. But mama cat was in no apparent hurry for motherhood. She'd simply gaze at me with the cryptic look that only a cat can give. It was unnerving.

One full week of fruitless anticipation later, mama cat was still kittenless and I was a bleary-eyed mess. I figured it would be smart to try and forget my feline worries for a while. As luck would have it, we'd been invited to a family swimming party. I imagined myself lounging at a pool all day, the perfect tonic for jangled nerves. Sure enough, the afternoon of sun and water worked its magic. Even when we got home, I felt boneless as a rag doll. Jessica made a beeline for the phone. I ambled along behind her, reminding myself to look in on mama cat before I collapsed.

Inside the room, there was no sign of a cat. But I wasn't alarmed; she was probably sleeping. I tiptoed over to the box and took a peek. Nestled deep inside the makeshift bed, I found conclusive proof that mama cat was no slacker.

My remaining fears evaporated the instant I proclaimed the news. "Jessica, we have kittens!"

I counted four black and gray squirming balls of fur. Each one was meticulously clean. They made little mewing sounds while their tiny paws pushed to scoot them toward their mother.

"Good job, mama cat," I told her. By golly, Carmen was right. Cats did know what to do.

Jessica raced in to see the new arrivals. I suppose it was all the excitement that prompted mama cat to stand ... and that revealed a fifth kitten. It looked exactly like the others, with one notable exception—mother and baby were still attached by the umbilical cord. I watched in horror as the smoke-colored newborn dangled upside down, crying in protest. Mama cat shot a look my way, her eyes round as beach balls. The message was clear enough. But just how did one go about detaching mother and baby? I knew it was a job that required someone with a cool head. Definitely not me.

"Jessica, call the emergency clinic." I hoped my manner exuded calm authority rather than the rising panic I felt by the time she handed me the receiver.

Within two rings I heard a man's voice. "Animal Emergency Clinic. May I help you?" A direct connection to God couldn't have been any better.

"My foster cat had kittens, and one of them is still attached to her by the cord. What should I do?" Realizing my voice was about two octaves higher than usual, I cleared my throat and waited.

The man sounded assured—bored even. No doubt he was accustomed to dealing with hysterical, know-nothing midwives.

"Is there hemorrhaging?"

"No."

"Signs of distress?"

"No." If you don't count having a kitten dangling from you as distressful.

"Then take the cord and pull . . ."

That didn't sound hard. I cradled the phone between shoulder and ear and with two fingers grabbed the membrane, which felt dry and flat as a rubber band. Jessica stared. The motherly part of my brain hoped she wouldn't be too upset by the crisis.

On the other end of the phone my savior's voice continued, ". . . but don't pull too hard, or you could cause internal damage to the mother. And pull by the cord, not the kitten, or you could jerk out its intestines." At least I think that's what he said. At that point my focus had slipped.

I felt clammy beads of moisture gather on my forehead as I gave the first infinitesimal pull. Nothing happened. A deep breath later, I tried again. Still nothing. Mama cat was beginning to look annoyed.

"This isn't working," I finally croaked into the phone.

The man sighed deeply. "Bring them to the clinic."

The thought of packing up a cat with her four and a half newborns was daunting. Yet, I supposed letting mama cat go through life with a dangling kitten was not a good option either.

Jessica tapped my arm. "Let me try."

Before I could warn her of the dire consequences of one wrong move, she reached over and in a single swift tug neatly separated the two. My stomach churned while I waited for signs of impending doom. Instead, mama cat serenely settled back into her bed while four kittens rooted against her to nurse. Jessica pushed the fifth baby into position beside the others.

The voice on the forgotten phone line came back to life. "Ma'am? Will you be bringing in the cats?"

"Uh, never mind. We're fine now."

And we were. Jessica beamed with pride, and I know my own face mirrored hers. I realized she'd tugged more than one motherly tie that evening. As we watched the peaceful scene together, suddenly my youngest didn't seem quite so young anymore.

By focusing on fears of what tomorrow might bring, I'd nearly spoiled the miracle of today. Now, I'm not certain a compulsive worrier ever truly reforms, but thanks to my daughter and a little gray cat, I figured it was time to try. When mama cat's drowsy gaze found mine, I could swear she nodded in approval. Then her eyes closed, and she began to purr.

—*Pat Wahler*

Confessions of a Naked Cat Lover

My secret was bound to come out sooner or later, so I might as well confess here and now: I'm a dog person who fell in love with a cat. Yes, it's true. And if that weren't bad enough, the cat is no ordinary feline. It is quite possibly the ugliest cat in the world. How did this happen? Even the most ardent dog lover will occasionally admit to a pang of warmth for a fluffy little kitty or a flirtation with a perfect purebred, such as a Persian (they do resemble Pekingese pups), but I had to fall for a cat so unattractive that even cat lovers have been known to recoil in horror. I fell in love with a rex.

This is no sexy Rexy, but rather a naked, scrawny Cornish rex with features resembling an alien from outer space. No exaggeration or hyperbole necessary, this may be one of the most unattractive felines in the history of catdom. So why do I find him so irresistible?

Love is blind. Belle married the beast, and I adopted the rex. While Belle's beast became a hunk, my cat-prince is still hiding his inner charm under a carcass of nearly naked flab. If I had fallen under the spell of a tuxedo tabby or a slinky Siamese, it might have been understandable, but a fixation on a furless feline freak is hard to explain.

I knew nothing about the Cornish rex breed when I began the odyssey that led to the cat connection of my life. I was simply looking for a new companion. My little Chihuahua was reaching senior status and wanted nothing more than to sleep in the sun all day. That was fine with me, but my children understandably wanted a pet they could play with.

Being a dog person, I first thought to get a puppy. But then I was worried a puppy might upset the Chihuahua. I also wasn't looking forward to months of new housebreaking discipline. The natural cleanliness and independence of felines convinced me that a cat would be the best choice.

Just as I had determined that puppy energy would be too stressful for my senior dog, likewise, I vetoed the idea of a kitten. With all the wonderful adult cats in the world waiting to be adopted, I knew we would have no trouble finding the right cat, not too young, not too old, to fit in perfectly with our family.

We went around to all the local shelters and carefully read the posted information cards and greeted the friendly paws reaching through the cages. One of the shelters had a huge cat room where the residents roamed free. There were nearly a hundred feline friends living together in perfect harmony (except for the occasional hiss here and there). It was the perfect place to find the perfect cat—and the perfect place to find out that we were allergic to cats! Because we were free to move among them, play with them, and hold them, the allergy symptoms were suddenly running as wild as the kittens. My youngest daughter and I discovered we had a problem that day. My oldest daughter was immune and didn't want to leave without a new furry friend. We went home empty-handed.

After that, we probably should have given up the idea of ever getting a cat, but visions of kitty plums danced in our heads. I can't recall exactly who it was that first mentioned a Cornish rex along with the misleading phrase "hypoallergenic," but I was off and running to look it up on the Internet. As I would later find out, too late, not only are Cornish rexes not hypoallergenic, they tend to aggravate allergies because of exposed dander.

I soon discovered Cornish rex rescue sites with adult cats available for adoption. I narrowed my search to locations within driving distance of my home. Only one cat was available nearby, and even he was out of state, but the drive was less than two hours away, so it would be worth the effort. It was a gray and white male about three years old. He sounded purrfect.

I quickly contacted the Humane Society that had posted the listing. I was told he was still available, but if I was interested I should hurry, because a waiting list was bound to form. (I later learned that Cornish rex cats sold by breeders can cost as much as a thousand dollars!)

I made plans to drive out to meet Rex the next morning at the crack of dawn. He was being fostered in a private home by one of the shelter workers who kindly took in overflow cats when the shelter ran out of space. During the long drive, the kids were quiet as mice, which seemed appropriate, given their eagerness to meet the mysterious cat they hoped would become their new playmate.

Upon entering the rex's foster house, I never would have guessed that nearly twenty cats were being sheltered there, because everything looked and smelled so clean and fresh. Felines were curled up here and there, quietly and inconspicuously relaxing while they awaited relocation. Only one cat was locked up behind a closed door, and the meowing was loud and long. If this had been a mystery story, the clues and foreshadowing were being laid out like pieces of a puzzle that I was too distracted to see.

I was told the lockdown cat was the very Cornish rex I had come to see. He was isolated for his own protection, because the other cats were picking on him. That certainly tugged at my heartstrings, but I couldn't help noticing that all the other cats seemed so mellow. All thoughts left my head the moment the door was opened and Mr. Rex was revealed. Skinny, scrawny, long, lanky, and bald. The strangest cat I had ever laid eyes on. A sphynx must have sneaked into the cattery somewhere along the line, because this boy was naked down to the pink skin covering most of his body. No matter. It only added to his unique charm. He went home with us that day. It was kismet. Or so I thought.

Within less than twenty-four hours, all the Cornish rex secrets were revealed. Although there was no fur to fly, our allergies took off in high gear. Dander wipes and endless hand washing would become part of a daily routine.

And I soon discovered why Cornish rex are referred to as "monkey cats." They seem to literally fly from room to room, wreaking mischief and havoc wherever they go. No shelf is too high, no surface too narrow. Things go crashing on a daily basis.

As for the natural cleanliness of cats, the Cornish rex are too busy having fun flinging kitty litter far and wide. Everything is a toy to a rex, so adjustments must be made. I now have a small plastic swimming pool in the basement to help contain the litter box mayhem.

Independence? That's for ordinary cats. No lap dog ever clung to his master with the tenacity of the Cornish beast. Velcro or Leech would make appropriate names for a rex.

The good news: rex cats are playful. Very playful. The bad news: our cat's favorite game is crisscrossing full-speed underfoot as we attempt to walk downstairs. People with bad vision, weak ankles, trick knees, balance problems, hip injuries, or heart conditions should think twice about getting a rex. In fact, anyone with common sense should think twice.

It's been seven years since we adopted our Mr. Monty Rex. Skinny and scrawny is now chubby and flabby but still as naked as the day we brought him home. Thinking back on that fateful day, I can now say with affectionate humor that I understand why his first family didn't exactly send out a dragnet to find him after he ran away. And I now know why the cats at the shelter were picking on him: he was undoubtedly driving them crazy!

But we love him.

—*Eileen Mitchell*

Creepy Cat

I know it's horrible to admit in a cat lover's book, but I'm a dog woman who hates mice more than cats. I had to be sold on the benefits of having a feline in the family. It didn't really take much. One mouse in the garage and I said, "Okay. Get one."

I went and bought the paraphernalia. You know, designer cat food, cat bowls, litter box, litter, diamond-studded collar. Even a leash. We were going to train the darn cat. We live on ten acres in the Ozarks of Missouri, in a hollow, or "holler" as people around here say. We couldn't let the kitten out without supervision and a leash, even for yard explorations. It was an indoor cat. Or that was the plan, anyway.

Princess, a skinny, striped girl who looked full grown and like she should be hungry for mouse snacks, arrived at our house when she was six months old. It took us all of about an hour to realize she pretty much had every bad cat habit in the book. She climbed: cabinets, curtains, people.

Our three-pound Yorkie, Mojo, nearly had a conniption when she decided his food was better than hers. And since she already outweighed him a few times over and had meaner hissing abilities, she left him no more than a few morsels—whatever he could snag and run away with, one kibble at a time. He barked. He bounced. But she won every single battle. (He's really a chicken dog.)

The situation worsened dramatically only two days after she got here. She went into heat. I'm not talking a well-behaved thing. Not just needy and a little purry, but rubbing roughly against every surface and person, squealing and squalling, begging for attention. Demanding attention. If you didn't reach out and pet her, she dug in her claws, arching up your leg or shirt front—if you were silly enough to let her on your lap—or tearing into my couch or drapes.

At first, it was funny; then it became disturbing. How long does a cat stay in heat? Answer: several days to two weeks, and they can cycle back in within two or three weeks. We needed to get her in to be spayed, but life was hectic. We lived thirty miles from the closest vet, and he was booked solid for two months.

Two months. That's only eight weeks. We could handle that. How many times could she cycle in before that snip date with the vet came around? Answer: another three times. I know—that seems way too much. But who controls that sort of thing?

We presumed she'd be all right as long as we didn't let her out on her own. Sounded good. Sounded easy as pie. Except, of course, the instinct to mate gets into a critter when they're in heat. Everybody knows that, and the cat didn't take long to figure out the front door was the escape hatch from her imprisonment. It was probably those darn leash expeditions to familiarize her with our property that got us into trouble. Sort of worked against us. And cat leash walking, well, if it can be done, we're not the ones to teach it. It didn't pan out for us.

What we soon learned, however, was that a cat is smarter than it looks. And just because a feline seems lazy doesn't mean it can't up and scat in a moment's notice—with someone saying, "Holy cow, what was that?"

Answer, of course: "Princess again, I think."

I'm dead serious here. Cats can pretend not to care if the door is open. But if it is open for more than three seconds or two inches, you're fighting fur at the gap. And, like a greased pig chase, there is no catching a cat that's side hopping and bounding worse than a drunken bunny in headlights once it gets out into the grass.

So, you might have guessed it, the cat got loose. She became an escape artist in record time.

At first, we panicked. Mostly because we were afraid she'd get hurt or lost. Then we realized that she had come to terms with our property boundaries, probably by virtue of neighboring dog territories being marked, which actually comforted us. We hadn't seen a cat in the hollow for years. That meant no toms around to get dirty with our little Princess.

And she didn't stay gone for long. But from then on, she'd slip out and take off for parts unknown. I'd panic and wail until she was found, sending five kids out as a search party, and swore we better not have kittens or the person who'd let her out was on death row and double toilet-cleaning duty. I'm really big on pet-owner responsibility and chore rewards for troublemakers.

The cat never slipped out through *my* legs. I just want to say that. I got smart in a hurry. I took her down the hall, cuddling and cooing with her, and locked her in the bathroom if I needed to go somewhere. That's where her cat box was, so I thought it was a good plan.

Well, one day, I arrived home from a shopping trip to hear, "Princess escaped again."

I squinted. "Please tell me she wasn't starting that squalling again."

We'd had a week or so of blissful, happy cat—in fact, so long that I began to panic. Had she gotten pregnant on her last Houdini deal?

"Yeah, well . . ."

There was no talking to me that day. If you were in the house, you weren't out looking for the cat, and I didn't want to hear whatever you said. I'm sort of snippy that way sometimes. Yes, she'd grown on me.

The kids came in. "It's starting to rain."

"Rain? You think our cat wants to be out in the rain? Get back out there!"

Then it thundered. Let them shudder. Suffering sometimes builds character.

They came running when lightning flashed. One streak, and they were in, and I couldn't turn them back out. The sky darkened. The night sunk to the looks of one of those creepy horror flicks, you know the ominous sky that sets up the scene for something bad about to happen.

"We're not doing television tonight," I said. "Or Internet." We have to unplug things like that so the lightning doesn't hit up the phone line and zap everything in the house.

"Is it because of the cat?"

"That and the storm. I am not happy she's out there."

Hours ticked by. I'm a writer, so I thought it was good the kids were forced into reading or going to their bedrooms to listen to their music.

It grew late. I got engrossed in a novel. I forgot about the cat. Sorry! I told you I was really a dog lover.

But, truth was, I felt horrible about losing Princess and about her being out in the storm. I even pulled on a raincoat and went out in search of her— yes, I admit it, while muttering, "A dog would have the sense to come in."

Our Yorkie quivered under the covers on someone's lap. But our fearless Princess stalked the world through high grass. Where could she be?

I was sick over it by the time I came in. I made some sort of comment about the property feeling like the House of Usher. Dark, ominous clouds hung overhead. Thunder crashed. I just knew some evil lurked in the woods, waiting for our little brat cat to make a wrong step.

I called and called, but that didn't matter. That cat doesn't come to her name. It doesn't suit her. She answers to a pointed finger; if she can see it, she'll come. She answers to the sound of dog kibble being poured (but not cat food; I cannot hear the difference). I tried pouring both at the front door but knew it was in vain with the rain pitter-pattering on the roof and porch. Finally, I gave up. I shut the door, dried off, and went to read my book again, wishing she'd snuck in when the door was open all those times and that someone would announce out of the blue, "I found her!"

But no, the cat was lost, outside in the cold rain, a victim of the dark and her own wanton wanderings.

I growled, "She better not get pregnant," to the first kid who slipped through the room.

"She'd better not get eaten by a neighbor dog," I warned the next.

"If I find who let her out, that person is cleaning the fridge," I snapped at the third.

The fourth and fifth heard the threats and stayed, like Princess, hidden from sight, not making a noise. Another hour ticked by. My concentration, though scattered at first, finally slid fully into the book I was reading. Totally engrossed, I sat on the sofa, alone in the living room. Everything was quiet.

Out of nowhere came a thump. Not just any thump. A thump at the front door. A hard thump. It made me jump, eyes wide and horrified.

Our front door is old. It has a tiny diamond-shaped window at eye level. Just one.

When the noise sounded, I flinched and looked, knowing something was watching me. Then she squalled. Princess had found her way home and leaped at the door, digging her claws in, screaming for attention.

The shock lasted two seconds, long enough for five kids to come running, all asking, "What was that noise?"

Princess's face peered in the diamond-shaped window. Upon seeing us moving, she cried louder, over and over. Gingerly, we opened the door. She clung, claws sunk into the old wood, splatted out like something in a Garfield cartoon. I kid you not. We had to peel her loose while laughing so hard we were crying.

For those who are left wondering if she got pregnant—no. Did she do it again? Every chance she gets.

That cat is crazy creepy sometimes. She picks the perfect moment to make us jump, like she actually knows it startles us. I have a theory on it, though. When she comes to the door and cries, nobody rushes to let her in now. She's a farm cat. She goes outside of her own free will. We've loosened up on that. If she wants out, she can get out. But nobody runs to let her in at the first meow unless she hits the door, clings on, and squalls at the window. That gets her instant attention and somebody petting her, laughing, and talking to her, telling her how clever and athletic she is. That is much preferred to the scathing look and "Brat cat!" she gets when she slips in at foot level after twenty minutes of noisy meows.

Either way, the dog goes crazy, and the minute the cat is on the ground, they're chasing through the house as Princess makes a beeline for Mojo's dish. He's getting a little gumption these days, though, and so my dog and cat play cat and mouse.

But even funnier than the cat's door attacks is the way she stalks the Yorkie. Creeping, creeping, neck stretched and eyes peeping, around the corner she slinks and waits until he finally assumes the game is over and lays down, eyes closed. Then she pounces, bounces, bats with clawless paws, and runs.

We finally wised up, by the way. If she's out and we want to find her, all we have to do is let the dog out. One sniff of the air and a yap, and he's off on her trail, chasing her until she circles back around to the house. If she wants in anytime soon, that creepy cat leaps for the door, sinks in her claws, hangs on, and yowls like there's no tomorrow. Works every time.

—Jennifer DiCamillo

Crystal Blue Persuasion

"Guess what!" Diane flashed her sweet smile, instantly putting me on my guard. When Diane smiled like that, it meant something was up—usually something I wasn't going to like. "I've come to Greensboro to get myself a cat."

Her Siamese, Kim, had died five years earlier, and a midlife career change had kept Diane's life too unsettled to provide a home for a cat. But now with physician assistant school behind her and a good job at a community hospital in a small town, she was ready.

I was happy for her. The only problem was she expected me to go with her to the animal shelter to pick it out. Besides the fact that I don't do shelters (I can't handle choosing just one animal, not knowing what will happen to all the rest), I also didn't know anything about choosing a cat. It's not that I didn't like them—some of my best friends have cats—but I was a dog person. With dogs always in residence, I had refused all chances at cat adoption, figuring they would fight like . . . well, cats and dogs.

Once Diane took a notion I should do something, though, I usually wound up doing it. I'm glad she never wanted me to pursue a life of crime. "No, your Honor, I did not plan to rob that bank. It was Diane's idea." Try telling that to the judge.

So there I stood on a cold, rainy Saturday in January, in the cat section of the county animal shelter. The room was clean, but airless, and it smelled of Lysol with an undertone of fear and hopelessness. Since there was no place to put our coats, we kept them on, and within minutes sweat popped out on my postmenopausal brow. I just wanted to get it over with.

Three tiers of cages lined the walls on either side of a small room with a narrow aisle running down the center. Only five of the cages were occupied, and it must not have been kitten season, because all the cats looked full grown. In one cage was a large black-and-white longhair that never moved. In another cage a sable-brown longhair sulked, looking like a disgruntled pasha. In another was an aggressive-looking ring-tailed gray tom. The most promising animal was a solid black male, but a note on his cage said "Hold." That left the only female, a much smaller cat than the rest. She was sort of all the colors: gray, brown, black, and tan, with a blue sheen.

When we stood by her cage, she stopped trying to open the latch long enough to give us an assessing glance. The contrast between the muted colors of her coat and her day-glow green eyes was entrancing.

Diane looked at the array and asked, "Which one do you like?"

It didn't matter to me, and I said so. I was just there to rubber-stamp her choice.

We'd been there several lifetimes (at least twenty minutes) when I finally asked, "Diane, do you see one you like?" I congratulated myself for having kept the irritation from my tone and my body language neutral.

"I don't know." Diane's forehead wrinkled.

This wasn't going well. I realized if I ever wanted to get out of there, I needed to get a little more involved. "Oo-kay. Do you want a male or a female?"

Diane looked undecided.

"Long hair or short hair?"

No response.

"How about color?" I asked in a last-ditch effort to narrow the field.

"I don't know. I just don't know."

Diane wandered from cage to cage, not lingering longer at one cage than another, as far as I could tell, and smiling unconsciously at an occupant.

"Maybe today isn't the day to get a cat," I suggested hopefully. "Maybe you should come back when there are more choices."

"No," Diane shook her prematurely white curls, "I want to get a cat today. Which one do you think I should take?"

It felt like she'd already asked me that sixty-three times. I found a tattered Kleenex in my pocket and wiped my brow.

"That's not for me to decide," I answered through gritted teeth. "It's not going to be my cat."

Diane resumed walking from cage to cage. Each time she passed in front of the little blue cat, a dainty paw shot out.

It wasn't like Diane to be so indecisive, nor, to tell the truth, was it like me to be so unopinionated. But I honestly wasn't cat-wise, and in matters of taste, Diane and I were very different. There was just one point on which we agreed perfectly: adopting an animal is a lifetime contract that has no backdoor clause.

Trying not to chew on the already frayed ends of my patience, I suggested we take the cats one by one to the get-acquainted room. But thirty minutes and four cats later, Diane had made no progress.

The nine-thousandth time she asked me which cat I would pick, I told her.

The black-and-white was pretty, but so passive you felt like you ought to check his pulse. The gray cat had a sneaky look that, combined with his aggressive stance, boded ill. The sable longhair had a permanent expression of supercilious disapproval. Maintaining an upbeat attitude wasn't easy for Diane. Having to see that cat's arrogant sneer every day wouldn't be good for her mental health.

But the little tabby . . . the faintest hint of a cat-smile adorned her muzzle, as if she pondered an intriguing question. In the natural light from the window of the get-acquainted room, the blue cast to her particolored coat was even more noticeable. She didn't shiver like the sable cat or fight to get away like the gray. When I held her on my lap, she settled right down and purred. I didn't know anything about cats, but that's what you wanted a cat to do, right?

I jettisoned my nondirective persona and spoke with all the authority I could muster. "This one, Diane. This is the cat for you."

Diane looked as confused and doubtful as before. "Are you sure?"

I put on my sincerest expression, looked straight into her eyes, and lied. "There's not a doubt in my mind. This cat is perfect."

Diane's bright blue eyes searched my face. "But do you like her? I mean, do you really, really like her?"

Diane was nobody's fool. I'd switched positions too fast, so now I had no choice but to brazen it out. "A pretty cat that wants to be held? And purrs? Um-hum!"

Diane studied me a moment longer, then smiled that sweet smile again and gave a short nod. "Okay, I'll take her."

Diane named the little cat Crystal. Her vet proclaimed her to be a blue tortoiseshell, saying her diminutive stature was typical of the breed.

I didn't see much of Diane through the spring, nor did her other friends, but in phone calls we noticed she was becoming progressively more erratic. By May there was unquestionably something wrong. In June she was diagnosed with *glioblastoma*, a swift and deadly brain tumor.

Surgery and radiation delayed the inevitable but damaged the language areas of her brain. Except for an aged mother, she had no family, so we moved Diane and Crystal back to Greensboro, into the garage apartment behind my house. At Christmas, Diane was well enough to fly home to Mississippi, but in January a new CT scan showed the disease was making inroads again. Diane died in March, but not before she helped me nurse my thirteen-year-old Brittany spaniel back to health following a splenectomy.

I moved Crystal's litter box to the upstairs bathroom of my house, but I'll admit it: I hoped some of Diane's cat-loving friends would volunteer to take Crystal. But weeks passed, and they replied to all my hints that Crystal was already bonded with me. Yeah, right. She looked at me like I was dumber than dirt when I tried to play chase the feather with her. Half the time, she threatened to bite me if I tried to pet her. She slept on my bed in the daytime but ran when I crawled in it. Several times a day, a frantic "come-save-me!" yip told me she'd cornered the dog. Again.

But I noticed that Crystal usually had business that brought her to the entry way—coincidentally, of course—just at the moment I got home. I don't know when she began to butt my hands if I didn't pet her quite enough. But I do remember the first time she purred as soon as I stroked her. Somewhere along the line she mastered love bites as delicate as an angel's kiss. And for reasons of her own, she stopped intimidating the dog.

Crystal still looks like a calico seen through a blue silk scarf. Her eyes are still day-glow green. But since that day in the shelter's get-acquainted room, she has never, ever cuddled in my lap and purred again.

When I remember that gray January day six years ago, I wonder who persuaded whom to pick out that little cat. But I do know the answer to one question. Yes, Diane, I do like Crystal. Really, really. I'm sure.

—Mary Margret Daughtridge

The Purrfect Cure

I jiggled the flag key in the lock. As I cajoled the door into opening, I heard the disgruntled meow of May's cat, Cleo, demanding breakfast, demanding the wonderful old lady whose lap he usually occupied. I glanced at the carved redwood sign above the door—May and Cleo—and shook my head over the way my mother-in-law adored this particular cat.

When the door finally opened, I asked, "Are you hungry, Cleo?" and laughed at the almost human cadence of his reply. I leaned over to scratch behind his ears. A sturdy Siamese/alley cat mix, Cleo's aristocratic ancestry was evident only in coloring and voice. He fell at my feet and lolled over onto his back. I stroked his stomach and throat before I rose and turned to the bright kitchen. May's collection of antique blue-and-white porcelain plates was a splash of color on the walls.

I grabbed a small can of gourmet cat food while Cleo wove figure eights around my jean-clad legs and increased the volume of his demands. I spooned the elegant fare into his bowl, refilled his special-formula dry food, and replenished his water.

Cleo abandoned my legs for his meal, and I returned to the front door to check the mailbox. It contained nothing but a few catalogues and some bills. I'd hoped for something personal, a letter or package, that might shake May from her lethargy.

The hysterectomy two weeks earlier had gone well. The prognosis was good; the tiny spot of cancer had not spread beyond the uterus. The doctor assured the family that, even at eighty-seven, May should be up and around by now. But she lay in bed, inert, unable to rouse the slightest bit of enthusiasm for living. When she was transferred to a convalescent home, she sank deeper into despair. The entire family rallied to bring back the sparkle to those aged eyes.

We made and delivered the juicy apple pie she loved. She thanked us and picked at it without enthusiasm. We sought out the latest novel by her favorite author, Rosamund Pilcher. It lay unread on her nightstand. We offered to bring her knitting, so she could finish the lovely pink mohair sweater she had started. She shook her head. Great grandchildren toddled in with ribbons in their hair and homemade get-well cards clutched in chubby little fingers. Nothing worked. Days passed, and May became more and more listless. The doctor was as puzzled as we were.

As I turned from the door, mail in hand, Cleo leapt gracefully to the top of the bookcase. He stared at me, awaiting the attention that he considered his due. I sank into the flowered chintz wing chair beside the telephone, and Cleo jumped to the floor and then up into my lap. He settled in with an appreciative rumble.

I dialed the convalescent home. "Please connect me with May Cooke in room 222," I said.

After the third ring, my mother-in-law's usually crisp voice came on the line. "Hello." She seemed distant, half-asleep.

"Good morning, May."

"Oh, hello, dear." Her voice faded off.

"How are you today?" I tried to be cheerful but sounded strident even to my own ears.

"About the same."

"I was calling to see if there was something you'd like. How about a strawberry tart from the French Bakery? How about your knitting basket? You could work on that beautiful pink sweater."

"No . . . nothing." There was an odd resignation in her voice. To me it said, *I may never eat a strawberry tart or knit again.*

I didn't know what to say.

"How's Cleo?" May asked.

"Purring loudly at the moment, because he's in my lap. But he misses you." I scratched Cleo's cheeks, and he closed his eyes in pleasure.

"Just as long as he's okay."

"He's fine. I'll be by for a visit as soon as I water your geraniums. They're at their peak of bloom. Gorgeous."

"That's nice."

"Good-bye, May. I'll see you in a few minutes."

After hanging up, I let my head fall against the back of the chair. Cleo kneaded my jeans and purred. I felt helpless, unable to do a thing for this woman I loved so much. I knew that if nothing intervened, May would simply fade away. Finally, I set Cleo on the floor and walked purposely out the front door.

Candy-striped geraniums hung in baskets from the eaves and tumbled over the railings on the porch. I watered them and then returned to the living room, where Cleo had curled up in the pink mohair in May's knitting basket.

"No, Cleo!" I said sharply. "May would have a fit if she saw you in there." I tipped the basket, and Cleo reluctantly crawled out.

I went out the back door into the small, enclosed yard. May's neglected herbs hung their heads and the roses drooped. I made the rounds with the hose. The cool splash of running water and the serene beauty of my mother-in-law's garden usually refreshed me, but not today.

I was more distraught when I returned to the house to find Cleo once again snuggled in the pink wool. I took two quick steps toward the cat, intending to shoo him out and to put the basket away in the closet. But as I leaned closer, I was captured by the soft rumble of his purr. He slumbered peacefully, curled into a tight ball of sable and cream fur. Ever so gently, I eased two skeins of fuzzy pink mohair from beneath Cleo and spread them over him, concealing him from all but the closest inspection. Then I hooked my arm through the handle of the basket and opened the front door, a relieved smile beginning to tug at the corners of my mouth.

Ten minutes later I slipped into the convalescent home, past the aides at the desk, and carried the basket down the long hall to May's room. From her nest of pillows, her curly white hair limp around her pale face, May frowned as I set the basket on her bed.

"I don't feel like knitting," she said.

Cleo stirred at the sound of May's voice. He poked his head from beneath the pink wool, tumbling a skein onto the bed. He inspected May and the room and then leapt gracefully from the basket onto the bedcover. After exploring the bed, he composed himself in May's lap with a satisfied purr.

"What will the nurses say?" May inquired, her fingers stroking the soft fur of Cleo's neck.

"They'll never know. I smuggled him in. I'll just smuggle him out again." I heaved a theatrical sigh. "I brought him because he was so lonely without you. He needs you, you know."

Her face softened. She was near tears.

Once on the subject, I couldn't seem to stop. "He's not eating much. I've tried every brand of gourmet cat food. He turns up his nose at them all."

May clutched Cleo to her chest. "I thought you said he was fine."

"I was trying to reassure you so you wouldn't worry." I shrugged, hoping my karma wouldn't suffer from little white lies. "I decided you should know the truth."

When I departed with Cleo in the knitting basket, my mother-in-law sat propped upright in the bed. She was ringing the nurse.

That afternoon May informed her doctor that she was needed at home to care for her cat. By evening she had badgered him into releasing her the following morning. She finished the pink mohair sweater at home with Cleo purring in her lap.

—Ann Newton Holmes

A Star-Crossed Romance

"Pirate, come on, get away from the window. Lamb chops for dinner tonight." I waved the plate of tantalizing morsels in my cat's direction.

At sixteen pounds, Pirate had never said no to food before. In fact, I'd once found him in the den, rolled down on his spine, belly exposed and hind legs extended, purring to himself after a meal of filet mignon. This boy liked his food.

Worried now, I went to pick him up and carry him to his plate. Something, I thought, had to be wrong. Before I hefted him, I pulled back the lacy curtains and looked outside. I didn't see anything. I set Pirate down in front of his dish. As soon as his four paws touched the floor, he ran back to the window. Perplexed, I went outside.

A tiny silver-striped head popped up from the center of the lirope in my front planter. Reaching in, I picked up an adorable silver tabby with the biggest front paws I'd ever seen. I guessed her age at six months. I counted her toes. She had six. Five fully developed, a sixth in between the thumb and index finger. Yep, this kitten had mittens.

I buried my face in her soft fur, and she began to purr. "Okay," I murmured into her fur, "let's see if you can get along with Pirate." I set her down just inside the door and braced myself. Pirate never wanted anything to do with any other cat. He was the only declawed cat I'd ever owned, and his outside wanderings were restricted to the end of a leash. Any cats with the nerve to invade his territory found themselves on the business end of his hiss. I really had no idea how this would work out.

Pirate walked up to the kitten, sniffed her, bumped her shoulder, and pushed her toward the kitchen. Fascinated, I watched him show her his dish and sit next to her while she devoured his lamb chop bits. Clearly, love at first sight! Again, he walked up to her and bumped her shoulder. This time he led her around the house, pointing out such areas of interest as the litter box and the kibble and water bowls. Tour finished, he lay down next to her and began to groom her.

It astounded me that Pirate had adopted this little girl. It frightened me too. Who knew what illnesses she had that could spread to Pirate? A trip to the vet for a checkup and a quick fix, and I brought my girl, now named Starlight, home.

The vet gave her a clean bill of health. That night she began to bleed from the mouth. Devastated, I called the vet, sure the anesthesia tube had nicked her esophagus during surgery, and rushed her back. Her little mouth and tongue were completely blistered. The blisters were breaking and bleeding. They put her on life support and told me she had a congenital illness triggered by the surgery. Whether she lived or not depended on her willingness to eat on her own once they removed the feeding tube. They also warned me that, although she wouldn't be contagious, if she lived, I'd have to keep Pirate separate from her while she recovered. The vet suggested he might try to attack her while she was weak.

I brought Starlight home three days later. I'd prepared a room just for her and made sure Pirate had no access. As soon as she returned, he pawed and meowed outside her door. I could hear her weak cries in response. Fearful Starlight couldn't withstand an attack, I was determined to keep them apart. On the second day I had her home, when I opened the door to feed her, Pirate shot in under my feet and raced for his little sister. He curled his body around her and began to groom her, covering her from head to toe with tender licks and refused to budge when I tried to get him out of the room. Starlight, contentedly surrounded by cat fur, slept pressed against his ample stomach.

Starlight fully recovered. The vet credited her quick recovery to Pirate's care. Love clearly conquered all. Pirate, it seemed, had signed on for sickness or health.

Two months later, in the middle of the night, Pirate suffered a seizure. Starlight woke me when it happened. She jumped on the bed and kept batting my face until I woke up and paid attention. I rushed him to the twenty-four-hour vet. Pirate never recovered. I often wondered if he knew of his illness and chose Starlight to replace him so I wouldn't be alone. Starlight sat at the front door for two days, refusing to eat or drink. She slept curled at the base of the door and hissed at me every time I passed her. I had taken him out through the front door. Somehow, she held me responsible.

Starlight is sitting on my lap as I write this. She just turned twelve, and now weighs in at sixteen healthy pounds. I have two other cats in the house, both boys, but Starlight refuses to give her heart to either one. She remains aloof and, I think, still in love with Pirate.

—Kim H. Striker

Smoky's Journey

Shortly after we adopted two children, ages seven and five, to love and take care of, we adopted two kittens for them to love and take care of. A local farmer brought us two males from a litter of half-Siamese kittens. Because of their mixed breeding, they both had deformed tails. We named one Smoky, because of his smokelike gray coloring. His tail was shorter than normal and oddly kinked, so that when he raised it, it looked like an arthritic finger. The other gray kitten's deformity was worse. His tail was full-length but bent back over itself in a Z shape. We were going to name him Zorro, but when he jumped out of a cardboard box and got his tail hung over the edge, preventing him from getting loose, we realized the deformed tail was dangerous to him. We had it removed, and he became Bob, for the bobbed tail.

Smoky and Bob grew and blended in with the family, along with the children. We bought a camper and taught the cats to enjoy riding in it. That was a good thing, because shortly thereafter we moved from far northeast Colorado all the way across the state diagonally to far southwest Colorado. We packed two kids, two cats, and all the belongings that didn't go into the moving van into the camper and drove over the mountains to our new town. My husband had signed a teaching contract and made a deal on a house.

When we arrived, we found out the house deal had fallen through. We looked and looked but could find no houses for sale in our price range. Rentals were almost impossible to find in the rapidly growing tourist town. School was about to start. Another teacher came to the rescue and allowed us to park our camper in his driveway. His wife didn't like cats or kids, so I spent a lot of time trying to keep all four from annoying her.

School started, and the kids had to register with no address. I began to understand how homeless families must feel. My husband had to grade papers and do lesson plans sitting in the driver's seat with a flashlight, while I tried to keep the kids and cats under control in the back.

We didn't want the kids to have to change schools again, but I began to despair of finding a house that would work for us. After several weeks of living like squatters, a for-sale sign went up on the house across the street. *We're going to get that house*, I vowed, *whatever it takes*. It took talking the seller down in price and borrowing money from my mother, but we finally had a place to move into, and the kids and cats had room to roam and play. There was a nice big elm tree in the backyard that all four liked to climb. One day I looked out and saw my daughter standing in the crook of the elm with the two cats on each side of her. I went outside.

"What are you doing?" I asked.

"Trying to get up my brave to jump down like the kitties do," she said. And then she did, landing on her feet just like a cat.

While teaching the cats to ride in the camper had been a good idea at the time, we found it had a down side. They loved to get into vehicles, and when anyone left a car window open, it wasn't long before they were inside. Our neighbors got used to checking for them and shooing them out before they left for work, but I worried that some day a stranger would unknowingly drive away with our cats, never to return. Sure enough, one fine summer day Smoky disappeared. We called and searched, to no avail.

The kids were heartbroken. They'd already had so much loss in their lives.

"Maybe he went to another foster home," Jerry said sadly, a concept he knew only too well.

His sister, Terry, added, "I hope he gets adopted by a nice family."

"I'm sure that's what happened," I said, not at all sure but willing to grasp any straw offered.

Gradually, the tears subsided and we all got used to Smoky's absence, even Bob. He became king of the house, the only pet, pampered and adored by all. In fact, I doubt if he missed Smoky very much. But the rest of us did. Things just weren't the same with only one cat. Someone's lap was always empty.

Six months later, on Christmas afternoon, the kids were playing with their new toys and my husband with his. My mother had given him a free-standing fireplace, which he was in the middle of installing. I was just starting to pick up the piles of wrapping paper and ribbon scattered all over when I heard Bob scratching on the front door to come in, as he always did. He'd gotten fat and lazy and didn't like to be out in the cold snow for long. I stepped over a piece of stove pipe to open the door and felt the cat brush against my leg as he came in. Then I heard yowls and hisses from the couch as—Bob?—reacted to the intruder. I looked down to see a gray cat with a raised, crooked tail—Smoky, a very scrawny, bedraggled Smoky—still rubbing against my legs.

The kids were yelling, "Smoky, Smoky!" as the cats raced around the house, chasing each other over the pieces of stove pipe and through the piles of Christmas paper in a chaos of celebration. Finally, I was able to pick up Smoky, over his brother's loud protests. The pads of his feet were bloody and worn thin, and he was skin and bones—not to mention very dirty. But oh how loud his purr was! How I wished he could talk and tell us his adventures. Where had he been? How far had he walked? What dangers had he faced? How did he find the way? Some things we just can't understand, and the force that brings an animal back to the family who loves it is one of them.

Smoky recovered nicely and regained his weight, although he never got as fat as Bob, who, after a few days, decided to accept him again. We often hear about how loving and loyal dogs are and how haughty and independent cats are. Well, maybe it was just a desire for free food and familiar surroundings that brought Smoky back, but somehow I doubt it. I think he missed us and got up his brave to make the long journey home.

—Jean Campion

Say What? The Serious Business of Naming a Cat

"I just want to be sure this is Buttercup." The vet tech unzipped the carrier and out popped a gray head.

"Oh yes, that is our Buttercup," I assured her.

"Well, we have a yellow tabby back there and . . ."

I had forgotten about the visual discrepancy between Buttercup's name and her gunmetal-gray color. Ever since I brought her home from the shelter, I've found myself apologizing for her name. It's the one she came with. I thought perhaps a child had named her, and I wanted to honor that. Of course, it's certainly possible she and one of her shelter mates traded names, leaving, someplace in this city, a yellow tabby named Charcoal.

Buttercup has kept mum on the subject, but I've noticed she never comes when I call her, so maybe she, too, thinks it's a bad match.

As for myself, I never thought much of mine. "Patty," as I was called growing up, sounded too plain.

"I wanted something everyone could spell," my mother told me.

True, I could spell my name at an early age. I found out later, however, that my father had named me after a jazzy piece of music popular at the time, "Patricia." As an adult, people at work started calling me Pat, and I went with it in a last-ditch effort at sophistication. Eventually I learned to appreciate the simplicity of it. And, unlike being named after a famous person, Pat doesn't carry the burden of my parents' expectations, except their modest hope that I could spell it, which I can.

It's hard not to put your own stamp on something you're naming, whether we're talking about kids or cats. One morning, a gal came into the office with a box of kittens she had found abandoned by the curb. As we weren't employed at the animal shelter, where such a find is sadly all too common, her box of kittens caused quite a stir. I left work that day with my purse in one arm and a yellow tabby in the other.

Now Buttercup would have been an apt name for my yellow tabby—perhaps a bit feminine for a boy, but at least not an obvious disconnect between name and appearance, since you would have to get pretty nosy to find out more information about the cat. But it never occurred to me to name him Buttercup or Butterscotch or Butter or any such color-coded name. I wanted a name that meant something to me, and I decided on the name Eli, after the Old Testament prophet. (It's easy to spell, too.) I'm not sure whether Eli's name elicited admiration from people for my originality and biblical savvy or a vague "Huh?"—but Eli was a memorable cat. His creative bathroom habits left the aroma of his presence long after he was taken up to kitty heaven in a chariot of fire.

After my creative fling with Eli, I left the naming to others. Callie, who came with Buttercup, retained her shelter name. A lot of people have a Callie, which is okay. A lot of people have a Pat, too, and that's okay. Easy to remember, easy to spell.

Then there's Smokey. My brother-in-law, who lives next door, named her Smokey when he saw the black/brown/gold/gray torti streaking across our yards one summer. When I opened my back door, she streaked right in and she hasn't budged since.

Now, the star spellers among you might well ask, "Why the 'e'?" That's because, when I filled out the vet's form, I put an "e" in Smokey. I didn't think it looked right, but neither did "Smoky." At home, I looked it up in the dictionary and found "smoky." Then I looked it up on the Internet, beginning my search with the bear—Smokey, that is.

The white cat with a gold cap and gold tail appeared in the newspaper one morning—and several days later appeared in my house. Her shelter name was Indy, which she kept. Maybe she was born on Independence Day. Or perhaps she lived in a household of racing fans. Or maybe in her younger days she ran laps at 220 mph. I don't know, but I can say Indy comes racing when she's called, particularly if I have a plate of food in my hand.

The white cat with a silver cap and silver tail showed up in the neighborhood last spring and stayed for the summer, mostly at my sister and brother-in-law's house. They didn't want a third cat. I didn't need a fourth. We did everything we could to find this friendly cat a home. Neighbors at the end of the street named the cat Princess—a fitting name for such a regal-looking animal—but they couldn't take Princess in because of their dog, Cosmo's, snippy veto, which tells you who makes decisions at their house.

As weeks passed I became concerned about the prospect of finding a litter of white kittens with silver markings in my vegetable garden. I volunteered to take the cat to the vet—who pronounced Princess a neutered male. Well, I didn't need to worry about kittens in the cabbage patch anymore. I named him Snowy, with no "e," because even I know how to spell

Snowy. My brother-in-law calls him Bob. Snowy Bob spends most of his time at their house.

T. S. Eliot had it right when he claimed, "The Naming of Cats is a difficult matter." As anyone who has read *Old Possum's Book of Practical Cats* or seen the Broadway play *Cats* knows, Eliot had a way with names. Case in point: Jennyanydots, Growltiger, Rum Tum Tugger, Mungojerrie, Rumpelteazer, and Old Deuteronomy. "Rum" and "Old Deuteronomy" are the only names recognized by my spell-check program, so if Eliot added an extra "e" to any of those other names, I wouldn't know and neither would you. That's a good way around the whole issue of spelling.

You have a lot to think about if you're faced with the challenge of naming a cat. If you want to keep it simple, though, I suggest one of these options:

- Take whatever name he or she comes with. If it's wrong, it's not your fault and the cat won't come after you seeking revenge.
- Ask your mother to suggest a name that's easy to spell.
- Ask your father the name of his favorite song.
- Find out what your brother-in-law calls it.

—Patricia Mitchell

Taming Miss Jazzy

According to the vet, our three-year-old cat, Jazzy, is obsessive-compulsive. She chews the end of her tail until it looks like a fountain pen dipped in an inkwell. She bats her grayish-brown paws at strangers and attacks their knees and ankles. Jazzy is more guard dog than cat. Rather than hide under the bed when friends call, she waits at the front window, a mini-tiger with tabby stripes and green eyes and claws out.

Recently, a painter knocked at our door. Jazzy flung herself at him, hissing and spitting like Taz from the Bugs Bunny cartoon. When I tried to intervene, she hissed and spat at me, too, her eyes black and dilated. Embarrassed and unnerved, I apologized and shooed Jazzy upstairs with a pillow. A little while later, before starting to work, the painter glanced around nervously and asked, "Where's that cat?"

Jazzy has thrown fits at a handyman, a mover, and several friends of our thirteen-year-old daughter, Juliana.

In a strange reversal, our cat is affectionate with us, her adoptive family, except in those instances when she feels threatened at seeing an unfamiliar face. She cuddles on our beds and is a fixture on my desk. She's friendly with our regular pet sitter and the girl's mother. She eats well and uses her litter box. She's trim and active, almost the perfect cat, except for those sporadic, unpredictable attacks.

That is why we've put her on meds. Jazzy is now part of the new Prozac Pet Nation—dogs, cats, and even horses on anti-anxiety drugs. Our vet prescribed amitriptyline, generic for Elavil, starting with five milligrams a day, which Jazzy took for a month. Each day we watched for signs of change, relief from her obsessive-compulsive symptoms. We praised our cat and petted her even more. To our disappointment, over that month Jazzy remained hissy at strangers and continued to gnaw on her tail. The vet doubled the prescription of amitriptyline to 10 milligrams; now we wait for more positive changes.

It wasn't always like this.

The beginning, like all love stories, began with hope and a dream. For years, Juliana begged us for a cat. William and I put it off. Our condo was too small. I didn't want to trip over a litter box in the kitchen or leave a sandy mess in a bathroom or near the front door. Cat-box odor was the deal-breaker.

Finally, we cleaned out the tiny laundry room and made a space there, planning to surprise Juliana with a kitten on her tenth birthday. For weeks we examined, held, and petted dozens of potential pets at shelters, adoption clinics, and at homes of friends who owned mother cats with new litters.

William suggested a gray female tabby. "They make good lap cats," he said. "The ones I've seen are pretty gentle."

Our future pet had hefty competition, a legacy to endure. When I was twelve, my family adopted a docile gray-and-white kitten my father named Putti after the cherubs in Renaissance paintings. William previously owned a cat, Sweet Pea, who lived up to her name.

We both kept a lookout for a gray female tabby, but to be thorough, we considered other cats too. A pair of black male kittens—too wild! Older cats at an adoption clinic—health issues! Shelter kittens that turned out to be feral.

After a month-long search, we found what we thought was the perfect kitten: an eight-week-old Torbie (a tortoiseshell and tabby mix) in a cage at a local Humane Society. Alert and friendly, she had white markings and an adorable half-orange, half-gray face. The kitten's distinctive feature was a pair of ears almost as large as her frame.

A shelter worker handed William the tiny fur ball, who had been found on the street with her mother, a small gray cat. He held the kitten and played with her. By now, after an exhausting search, there was no surprise left for Juliana, only anticipation.

"I want this kitten," Juliana said. So did we.

We named her Jem Jelly Jazzlica after the characters in the musical *Cats*. Jazzy for short. Little did we know how well the name suited her.

At home, after a minor intestinal bug for which Jazzy was prescribed antibiotics, she became bold and fearless. She scaled furniture, arms, and legs, and pranced around the house with an arched back, her tail fuzzed out like a Halloween cat. We thought she'd outgrow her aggressive, kittenish tendencies. Over time, though, Jazzy's precociousness turned into anxiety. The sound of the doorbell made her put up her claws.

For a while I thought our home of thirteen years was the problem. "She's too cooped up in this little condo," I said. "There are no sun patches for her to lie in. She's climbing the blinds to get to the light." William agreed, but moving to a bigger house wasn't in our budget at that time. Letting Jazzy outdoors where she could expend her abundant energy was not an option either. We lived at the edge of a canyon where coyotes roamed and could be spotted at dawn on our street.

When Jazzy was a year old, we moved to a larger home a few blocks away that had windows and sun patches galore. *Jazzy will be happy here,* I thought. She was, for a while. When the novelty wore off, she became feisty again and suspicious of guests, especially men in workman's boots. She started to chew her tail.

"Maybe a man in boots frightened her when she was on the street," I told William. Or the unthinkable. I lowered my voice. "Maybe a man in boots did away with the rest of her litter."

"Maybe," William said.

I had read in a cat care book that kittens who aren't handled during the first weeks of life might not respond well to humans. We'll never know.

One thing is certain: Jazzy is a survivor, and that gave me comfort. My quirky, scrappy cat had had a difficult childhood. She was doing the best she could. I, too, have obsessive, perfectionist tendencies. I wondered whether I had inflicted them on Jazzy, had scrubbed the bathroom sinks with a little too much vigor.

Over time, I began to cringe when the door-bell rang. I'd place Jazzy on a plant shelf so she'd be at eye level and wouldn't feel threatened at seeing a stranger. I asked visitors to hang back and not pet her. If she seemed agreeable, I advised them to approach her cautiously. During parties, I locked Jazzy in our bedroom.

I started to fantasize about dogs, envisioning a cute little Pomerian who'd lick a guest's hand. But I knew Jazzy wouldn't tolerate a dog.

"Get a big dog," my friend Barbara suggested. "Jazzy might not fight if the pooch is bigger than her."

Fighting, flying fur. I was in over my head.

I briefly considered giving Jazzy up for adoption, but feared she might fall into the hands of a less-tolerant owner. An antisocial pet might wind up being euthanized.

I started to fantasize about—gulp (pet owner guilt trip)—the day Jazzy would be gone (of natural causes), and I could adopt another, friendlier pet.

"How long do you think Jazzy might live?" I asked William.

"She's a healthy cat," he said, "at least another ten years."

Ten more years of bad behavior, ten years of waiting. The stress on Jazzy's nervous system could not be good either. I had to do something.

I read a newspaper article about pets on meds: a dog being treated for separation anxiety that barked and tore up his owners' home when they were away, and a cat with some unspecified emotional problem that suddenly began to claw her owner. On a pet Web site I read a letter to a vet from a man who sounded like me. He wrote that his good-natured cat freaked out when guests came over and that he was at his wit's end about the bad behavior.

When I expressed my ambivalence about drugging my cat to Barbara, she said, "Do you want to live like this for another ten years?"

As if I had a disease. Maybe I did. Maybe I was codependent, a cat enabler, encouraging antisocial behavior. I envisioned the day when neighbors would refuse an invitation to lunch, make excuses when invited to a dinner party. I would be shunned, a refugee hunkered at home with a vicious pet.

That same morning I called our vet, who, after I described Jazzy's behavior in an office visit the year before, had suggested Prozac. I had laughed four years ago when my cousin Debbie told me her poodle was on Prozac. I wasn't laughing anymore.

"How will I get her to eat the pill?" I asked.

"Grind up the medication in her food," he said, "or put the pill inside a piece of cheese."

I tried stuffing the blue pill into a ball of cheese and then tuna. She ate the cheese and the tuna— but spit out the pill, intact, both times. I ground up the pill and mixed it into gourmet cat food, and after that into a small piece of shredded chicken. Each time, Jazzy ate the glob with the hidden medication once and never again.

I called the vet again.

"Open Jazzy's jaws and drop the pill down her throat," the receptionist said.

I pictured bared fangs. I imagined bloody scratches. Surprisingly, Jazzy allowed me to dose her this way. Every morning before breakfast I open her jaw and drop the pill down her throat. After, I offer a cat treat. So far, so good.

But I worry the meds will turn Jazzy into a listless slug, that the spark in her personality might vanish. Already she seems to have less interest in playing with her favorite catnip-filled mouse.

"It's a compromise," William said. "What can we do?"

Jazzy will need to undergo yearly blood tests, as amitriptyline might affect her liver enzymes, though research says the drug does not usually have long-term negative side effects on cats. With new habits and positive social interactions, our cat might even be able to discontinue taking the medication.

Will Jazzy become less obsessive-compulsive? The drug's effectiveness is not guaranteed. Our cat chews her tail less now, occasionally rather than every day.

She may never be a Putti or a Sweet Pea; maybe the bar was set too high. I hope she will be able to tolerate houseguests and handymen. I don't expect her to purr and rub on strangers' legs, just to sit calmly on the couch or a lap.

I asked the vet what would happen if Jazzy didn't respond to amitriptyline.

"We can try a combination of drugs," he said, "including Prozac."

Whether it's that medication or another one, I want to fall in love with my cat again, like that first day at the shelter. I want to get back that dream. Behind Jazzy's bad behavior is a sweet, unspoiled kitten.

Last week, Jazzy hissed at a neighbor who knocked at our door. Yesterday, when a friend of Juliana's came over after school, our cat eyed the girl but sat quietly as she passed by. For me, this is progress. Our cat's anxiety disorder has created a cockeyed silver lining in all the drama, drawing William, Juliana, and I closer together as we joke and strategize about how to help our nerve-ridden cat. We are on day 26, and counting, of Jazzy's new dose of meds.

What I did for love, I'd do again.

—*Allison Johnson*

Mr. Momma Cat

For a girl who grew up in the country, where she must have observed the habits of a variety of livestock and a succession of pets, Mama had some surprising inhibitions. I understand why she might have known minimally about the sex life of cows, since Grandpa's Jersey cow was walked down the road to a neighbor's farm when it was necessary to continue milk production. It is more difficult to comprehend why Mama sometimes professed not to know whether our cats were toms or tabbies. Perhaps her strong sense of privacy extended to felines, such that the indignities of inspection were not to be inflicted upon them. Another possibility is that she loved to create a humorous mystery.

When I was about six and my parents settled in as publishers-editors-reporters of a small weekly newspaper in northern Oklahoma, a special pair of kittens entered our lives. These purebred Persians had such long, thick fur that it hid all overt evidence of sexuality. The generous donor of these feline beauties admitted only that one was male and the other female. Mama named them Mitzi and Fritzi, and let the chips fall where they might. Dad merely nodded, accepting her name choices without offering any help with gender identification, despite being the son of a veterinarian.

In any case, both cats were supposedly "fixed," which made the names a moot point for the time being. That soon proved to be a myth. Mitzi grew to be half again as large as Fritzi, and it was Fritzi who deposited newborn kittens into Mama's shoes on the floor of her closet!

Mitzi was such a tom-about-town that the entire neighborhood soon knew his real gender. He also made a reputation for himself by climbing high into trees, where he would remain, howling, too scared to climb down. Once, he howled and yowled for three days and nights from the top of a cottonwood tree just outside our next-door neighbor's bedroom window. I spent most of those days beneath the tree, alternately calling to Mitzi and crying. Mama tried to coax him down by waving open cans of salmon back and forth, hoping the aroma of his favorite food would overcome his fear. Dad tried to reach him by ladder and failed. When Dad climbed onto the nearby roof, Mitzi clawed his way higher up the tree and his howls grew even more piercing. Finally, Dad called the fire department for help. Back then, it was not unusual for folks to call the local fire department for such rescues. Who else had the tall ladders and men unafraid to climb them to great heights? Today, that practice would most likely result in a hefty bill presented to the caller.

After Fritzi produced her four kittens, Mitzi became a model of deportment, a responsible feline spouse and hovering parent. As if she had declared, "Now, it's my turn to have fun!" Fritzi started wandering farther afield in search of catly delights, such as chasing butterflies across the street and teetering along fence tops. Although she regularly returned to feed her newborn kittens, Fritzi disappeared for hours at a time. Mitzi took over like a veteran kitty-sitter, and the kittens soon deferred to his benign authority. They loved to climb on and over him, tumbling around on him in play and nipping at his tail with their milk teeth, and to nap on top of his stretched out body. He tolerated their antics with dignified patience.

Mitzi was fond of lounging in a canvas-slung folding chair on our front porch. He would jump into it and stretch out his big frame. The kittens quickly learned to scramble up the wooden framework to join him. There, he would thoroughly wash himself and then each kitten in turn. Often, by the time he had licked three kittens to his satisfaction, his tongue would have "lost its spit," as Mama said. His eyes would droop, and soon he would be fast asleep, with three napping kittens sprawled across his back and the unwashed fourth asleep between his paws.

When the kittens were old enough to scramble down our front steps to play on the sidewalk and test the grass, Mitzi hovered around them like a nervous mother letting her children cross the street for the first time. Once, as the little troop frolicked on the lawn, Mitzi spied a bulldog coming down the street. When the dog spotted the kittens, it speeded up on its short legs. Mitzi rushed to grab the kittens by the scruffs of their necks and tossed them up the front steps to the porch. By then, the bulldog was running toward our house. Mitzi herded his young to the front screen door, startling them into alarmed hysterics that sent them clawing up the screen as far as they could go. Then he turned to face the canine menace.

Mitzi weighed almost sixteen pounds. With his long fur standing up in alert mode, he looked almost as big as the bulldog and was twice as fast with his curved claws. Launching himself off the porch like a missile and growling his fiercest, he landed on the dog's head with a quick slash of claws across the face that sent the dog running back to the street, shrieking and squealing. Never relaxing his attack, Mitzi was a whirlwind of claws and teeth atop the panicked dog. Finally, he jumped off the dog, and with a few more swipes with his razor claws, he chased the bulldog down the block. Satisfied, Mitzi sat down in the middle of the street to wash himself free of canine smell, while the bulldog continued running and yelping down the street.

Meanwhile, the animal commotion and my own shrieks brought Mama out. As she flung open the screen door, all the kittens scrambled higher and draped themselves over the top edge of the door frame. Being only five feet tall, Mama could not quite reach them from front or back, nor did she dare close the door on kitten paws and tails. All four meowed loudly in distress, turning themselves around and around as they clung to their precarious perch.

When she could be heard over my yells, Mama told me to hold the door open while she ran to get a ladder. It took some time for Mama to get each kitten to let go and be lifted to safety. A cat under rescue digs its claws into the rescuer, and Mama was bloody before all were safe. Mitzi ambled back to his favorite chair, where he sat down and watched the final res-cue with an expression of complacency, as if to say, "I've done my part, now you humans do yours."

We never saw the bulldog on our side of the street again.

We could not afford to keep six cats. Homes were found for the kittens, and Mitzi mourned and was bewildered as they vanished one by one. A few weeks later, Fritzi died. Mitzi acquired a new solemnity, often sitting for hours on Fritzi's grave in our back garden. He even stopped climbing trees. I started school that fall, and my parents worked long hours at the newspaper office. Mitzi must have felt lonely.

Whereas once Mitzi and Fritzi had slept under the covers at the foot of my parents' bed on cold nights (we always wondered how they breathed down there), now Mitzi climbed onto my bed and settled himself on top of my wool comforter to sleep. With his mate and playmate gone, his straying days ended.

To those who think of our feline friends as "only cats," without souls, my proof to the contrary is strong. They feel. They care. They love. They grieve.

—Marcia E. Brown

Brotherly Love

When my sister died suddenly in a car accident, many of us ended up sitting in a chair across from someone who was going to put our heads back on the right way. My mother, though, could find no relief from the seven stages of grief, until she finally found the right psychologist—for her.

The therapist did not talk about human emotions or behavior. Instead, he sat there very calmly and told her stories about animals. He talked about how, if an animal is hurt, other animals will come to help. We all thought it was a little strange, but his stories really did help Mom. She went back again and again, each time returning to us a little better than before.

I have two very unique cats. (These thoughts are connected; you'll just have to give me a minute.)

Sam and Oscar were barn cats, born of the same litter. This is, however, where their similarities end.

Sam is a very fluffy black cat who was two years old before he made his first sound. He is vain to the extreme, constantly preening and categorically avoiding mud and the outdoors. He is as dainty and affectionate as a pampered princess. If you sit down in my house, he will find a way to sit on you.

Oscar is mischievous and aloof. This scruffy, long-haired tabby enjoys sitting behind chairs or lying in the middle of the kitchen so he can hook your sock with his claws as you walk past. I think it is our stumbling and swearing he enjoys, because he also has an internal alarm clock that wakes him up every morning at 4:00. If he is in the house, he meows at the foot of my bed until I go downstairs, stumbling and swearing, to let him out. Of the 5,000 pillows and shoes I have lobbed at him at four o'clock in the morning, he has avoided all but one. He is the only cat I know that can stomp his feet.

Oscar is famous for going on walkabouts and is often gone for days at a time. So I scarcely noticed when he went missing for a few days. Even when my father-in-law said something about finding my cat stuck in the fence, it didn't really register—in one ear and out the other.

That night I went down to the basement and noticed Oscar curled up on the new La-Z-Boy. The next day I made two separate trips to the basement. Again, Oscar was curled up on the chair. I said something to him each time I walked past, and he lifted his head and meowed something in response.

On the third day, it was the same thing. "Holy cats, you're lazy! Why don't you go catch some mice or something? Go make yourself useful," I said as I walked over to him.

At that point, the stench reached my nose, but I had no idea what it was or where it was coming from. I kneeled down to pat my cat, and he was a bag of bones. My fat cat had ribs! I stood up and called Oscar to come with me and we'd go find something to eat. He meowed but refused to move.

I decided to be nice and returned with a saucer of milk and put it on the floor by the chair. Oscar lifted his head but did not move. *Okay,* I thought, *if he's going to be obstinate about it, I'll just put him in front of the dish in a maternal "eat that" sort of way.* When I tried to pick him up he made a noncatlike sound at the same time my hand found something wet.

What I found upon inspection was unreal. Oscar had no skin from the inside of his knee, up his belly and chest, to his armpit. Nothing. It was just muscle, bones, and wet stuff.

He never made a sound. He just looked at me. I brought the bowl up to him on the chair and laid it between his front feet. He licked slowly, carefully, and steadily. When it seemed he was done, I put the plate on the floor and went to find a box and my husband.

"That's one tough cat you have," the vet said. "But I can't do anything for him. There is no skin for me to sew together. The piece is missing."

"What can we do?" my husband asked.

"You could put him down."

"Is he going to die right away?"

"Well, he's missing half the skin on his underside. His chances aren't great. You should put him out of his misery."

"Look, he spent three days pulling his own skin off trying to escape from a barbed wire fence. Then he spent three days in our basement. I think he deserves a fighting chance."

"The best I can do is to give him a huge dose of penicillin and send him home."

"Sold."

Oscar made a grunting sound as the vet gave him the injection.

We decided the La-Z-Boy was ruined now anyway, so we might as well put him back there. I sat beside him, stroking him, reassuring and comforting him. That's when I noticed the stuff on the floor.

There was a little gray field mouse—dead, next to the chair. Not far away was a bunch of small chewed-up bones. Sam had been bringing Oscar food. All that time while we had been ignoring our injured cat, his brother had been taking care of him.

For the next week or so, we noticed Sam was never upstairs. He spent all his time hunting for food for his brother. Over and over, he came in the cat window in the basement with a dead mouse or bird, dropped it off with Oscar, and went right back out. All the while, we continued to bring Oscar milk and wet cat food, but that didn't seem to matter to Sam. He was determined to keep helping his brother.

One evening I went downstairs to double-check on our patient. There was Sam, grooming his brother. In a way, Oscar had never looked better. His fur (what he had left) was super clean and smooth. When he was satisfied with the job, Sam stretched out along his brother's back and went to sleep.

The next day when I went down, Oscar meowed a greeting at me and started to sit up. He was stretching his nose tentatively over the edge of the chair, so I helped him hop down. His skinned back leg was now shorter that the others and curled in slightly. He had to fight to keep his balance and figure out how to walk on only three legs. Slowly he made his way to the basement door, and I let him out. It was a sunny day, and I was so proud of my cat I sat down with him in the grass to see what he would do next.

He got nagged to death is what happened next. Sam came slinking out of the orchard with another mouse swinging from his mouth. He dropped the prize in front of his brother and proceeded to inspect every inch of the wounded cat. When he was satisfied Oscar was all right, he headed back into the orchard to continue his hunt.

For two weeks after Oscar emerged from the basement, Sam continued to hunt relentlessly. To this day Sam will wait patiently for the now healthy and mischievous as ever Oscar to finish eating out of the cat-food dish before he has one bite.

Animals know how to take care of each other. Feed him, keep him clean, keep him warm, and love him with all your might. As a community of people, if someone we know is hurt, physically or emotionally, we bring casseroles or send cards. If we are allowed, we touch, we hug, we listen, and then we wait. We gather together at funerals so we can circle each other's chairs, looking for a sign that the person in pain might be in need of a new mouse.

When my sister died we all circled my mother's chair, we all brought her mice. It just took a tender-hearted psychologist to convince her to eat one.

—*Allison Maher*

A Purrfect Match

At the age of four I was a normal little girl who loved animals and wished more than anything for a small, furry friend to keep me company. When I would ask for a kitten, my parents would always cite my father's allergies as the reason I could not have a cat. No kittens for Sarah on her birthday. No kittens for Christmas. No kittens at all. That didn't stop me from asking. Frequently. Every holiday that children are given presents, I asked for a cat.

The tension in our house was pretty high. My parents were always arguing about something. Even so young, I had enough friends at daycare whose parents were separated to see what was coming. I don't remember the talk my mother had with me the day my dad moved out, but she has told the story a thousand times.

With great dread, my mom sat me down to explain why my dad would be living in another house. She had her speech prepared; all the things she would say to mend a daddy's girl's heart. Before she could utter a word, I looked up at her with my dark eyes (she'd later decide the look was calculating) and asked her, "Are you and Daddy getting divorced?" She nodded, stammering a "Y-yes" and throwing up a silent thank-you to an overpopulated daycare and a sudden surge in Spokane's divorce rate. Without hesitation, as if I'd been planning for this moment for all four years of my life, I made an offer. "Can I get a cat now?"

She sat there dumbfounded for a moment (and secretly proud of her daughter's bartering skills). Thrilled not to have to pick her way through the minefield of that conversation, she quickly agreed. The bargain was struck. I was to have my heart's greatest desire. That is a grand thing for a little girl.

For the next few days it was all I could talk about, all I could think about. I was getting a cat. Me. I told everyone at daycare. I told everyone in line at the grocery store. I told anyone who would look at me for longer that two seconds that I was getting the kitten I'd "always wanted my whole life." I remember people smiling at me a lot.

The big day came with much fanfare. I leapt out of my brand-new big-girl bed, ran down the hall, and pounced on my poor sleeping mother. After break-fast, she loaded me into the little gray car, and we drove to a ranch-style house. The house I remember quite clearly, probably because I thought, even then, that it was ugly. It was small and salmon-colored with dark green trim, tiny windows, and too many shrubs in the front. It struck me as a dark place.

I don't remember any small talk, although I'm sure there was some. I don't remember what the mother looked like or much about her two kids, who were down the hall playing with a kitten and a bit of string. The mother cat, if I remember cor-rectly, was a calico. Very pretty and very watchful, she was sprawled on the floor in a lazy C, but her eyes were fixed intently on me, her tail flicking as she appraised me. Sitting next to her, almost as if wait-ing for permission to say hello, was the last available kitten. The cautious kitten was a sleek black with a white throat, chest, and belly, and four little white paws, like the rain boots in my closet. Her face was solid black, with not a trace of white. Her green eyes stared up at me, and my heart was hers. She was shy and timid as she took those first tentative steps toward me. She looked as out of place in that house as I felt in my own life. We were perfect for each other. On the drive home, as I held the tiny, mewl-ing thing close to my chest, I named her Boots.

We were a lot alike, Boots and I. We were content with each other, full of love. She followed me around all day and slept at my feet every night. She became my constant when life was unpredictable. I did my best to be hers, too; always ready with a bit of string when she was playful or a chin rub when she wasn't. I could tell her anything, and she wouldn't judge me or contradict me. She could bring me mice and moles and not get scolded. We understood each other. We were inseparable. For her whole life, Boots was the best friend a girl could ever ask for.

—*Sarah Wagner*

The Fleece Robe

My sister, Norma, has been a dog person for most of her seventy years. Although she doesn't dislike cats, they just aren't dogs. They don't have the personality or responsiveness of a dog, she's often claimed. Cats might be cute or funny or lovely (in their own way), but she wouldn't choose to live with one.

I'm as much of a cat person as Norma is a dog person. I've loved cats all my life and cannot conceive of living without at least one cat. I like their independence, playfulness, and elegance. When Norma and I decided to share a home in Albuquerque, New Mexico, we made adjustments, especially in the animal department. She brought her West Highland white terrier, Meggie, and I brought my two cats. The animals worked out their own relationships and learned to tolerate each other eventually.

On a windy, gray Halloween day I roped Norma into working with me at a cat show. It was a show for purebred cats, but the show also included cats from local rescue groups that were ready for adoption. During the day I discovered a tiny, seven-week-old, seal point Siamese-mix kitten who was waiting for a home. His gray-blue eyes scrunched tightly together when he opened his mouth wide in a loud "meow," telling everyone within earshot that he didn't want to be in a cage any longer. He stood defiantly with his short, stocky legs spread wide and his nose pressed against the wire, while cream and sable hairs sprung out in a halo around his body.

I decided on the spot to adopt him. Norma eyed him several times before agreeing, and the kitten came home with us, protesting all the way. He threw himself on his back and kicked at the sides of the carrier and bit at the wires of the cage door—all the while meowing in a howl that was too loud for his small body. By the time he got to the laundry room area, where he would spend his first few days adjusting to his new surroundings and the other animals, he was exhausted.

Every day Norma visited with him for a few minutes so he would become accustomed to her scent and so Meggie would recognize his scent on her clothes. On his third day with us, I noticed something was wrong with him. He seemed lethargic and wasn't eating well. I took him to the veterinarian the next day, and the news was not good.

After examining the kitten and doing a blood test, the veterinarian told me the kitten had feline panleukopenia virus, an often deadly disease common to unvaccinated kittens. Although they didn't realize it at the time, the local Humane Society had brought several cats to the show that had already contracted the disease. Now, the shelter had a panleukopenia epidemic on its hands. Few infected cats were expected to live. The shelter was allowing people to return any infected cat adopted from them, and any returned cat was humanely destroyed.

The veterinarian wasn't certain he could save our kitten, but he said he would try if I wanted him to. I agreed because I knew our kitten was a fighter and I wanted to give him every chance to live. The vet treated him with massive amounts of intravenous fluids and kept him overnight. Seeing the little guy with all those tubes running out of him and hooked to bags of fluid made me sad. When I brought him back home the next day, he looked like a bedraggled mop of fur, but he was breathing.

I was concerned about letting the kitten near our other animals for fear they would become ill. The veterinarian assured me it would be all right, because the other cats were current on their vaccinations and the kitten could not pass the disease to the dog.

Norma and I took turns sitting in the rocking chair holding the kitten, rocking him and talking to him. We tried to get him to eat and drink, without much success, but he liked being held. I told him that if he continued his fight to live, I would name him Rocky, after Rocky Balboa, the tenacious boxer Sylvester Stallone portrayed in the movie *Rocky*.

Norma wore a cozy white fleece robe every evening. Rocky fell in love with the robe. As soon as he felt it, he eagerly reached up to secure his claws in the fleece. He kneaded continually while working his way up the robe to Norma's armpit. There he hung, kneading and purring, for as long as she would hold him. He closed his eyes tightly together to better savor the pleasure of fleece under his claws and the warmth of her body next to his.

When he opened his eyes four days later, they looked brighter. He accepted a little of the baby food I had ready for him. From that slim beginning I knew he was going to be all right. His recovery was slow and steady with only a few minor setbacks. Our veterinarian was thrilled with this outcome, because the Humane Society lost eighty cats and kittens to the virus.

Rocky made up for lost time by eating everything I gave him. He began to put on weight and grow a little taller. But every night he crawled into Norma's lap, climbed up her robe, and stuck his little pink nose into her armpit, all the while kneading the fleece under his paws. I noticed that Norma smiled when she stroked Rocky and that she wasn't making him get off her lap until he wanted to go. He ventured off her lap periodically but scurried right back on before she got up. If she did want him to get off, he would meow and hold on tighter. Usually he won out.

One night Norma looked at me and said, "Rocky really is cute and funny, isn't he?"

"Yes, he is," I said. "And he's become quite fond of you. I think he believes you're his mother."

"You think so?" Her smile told me she was quite pleased at that thought.

A year went by, and Rocky still thought he needed to tuck his nose into Norma's armpit whenever she wore the white robe. I was sure she wouldn't be able to get rid of the robe, because he was so attached to it.

Rocky lay in her lap one night, kneading the soft robe and purring, with his lips curled into a cat smile. Norma looked at him and said, "I think Rocky might have turned me into a cat person. He's the only cat who could ever do that, but I think I'm hooked."

The conversion was complete. Rocky owns the singular distinction of converting my sister, the dog person, into a cat person. We just haven't told the dog.

—*Nancy Marano*

When the Time Is Right

The plane ride felt bumpy, but every bit of disturbance was inside me. I was flying across five states to see my widowed mom, hoping to somehow comfort her after her cat's death. When she'd lost my dad to cancer five years earlier, Genji, an orange-and-white ring-tail tom, became Mom's only companion. During those years, Genji followed her from room to empty room until they'd finally curl up together in that painfully large king-sized bed.

Over sixteen years of visits, I'd come to love Genji almost as much as Mom did. And I never got to say good-bye. My grief didn't matter, of course, not when I longed to help her heal by choosing another cat.

The drive to the Humane Society in a violent thunderstorm took us down unpaved roads. We were both nervous and edgy by the time we pulled into the parking lot. Fortunately, unlike the surrounding territory, the inside of the building seemed normal, if not welcoming.

Assuming Mom would follow, I rushed over to the cat cages. A sand-colored male with a muscular body nuzzled forward, clawing at the bars, trying to reach me. I petted him until the hefty gray in the next cage yowled for attention. I was wishing I had a third hand to respond to the pure white cat below my hips, when a pleasant young volunteer approached.

"Did you want to complete an adoption application?" she asked.

Absolutely. But I wasn't sure about a question on the application—*For what reasons might you return your pet to the Humane Society?*—and I turned to catch Mom's eye.

She wasn't watching me or looking over my shoulder at the application. Her focus was on the cages and cages of cats and kittens lining the walls. She didn't run over to them or say anything, but the faintest smile played on her lips. This was cat heaven, and Mom looked almost happy.

"Absolutely no reason to return a cat."

The volunteer smiled and invited us to explore. "There are more than 700 cats here. You'll find the right one for you."

Gently, I steered my mother toward the first of many corridors crammed with cages of cats stacked to the ceiling. Many cages housed two, even three cats. "C'mon, Mom. Let's try to find one that looks like Genji."

Both of us stopped walking when we approached the first cat room. Yes, a room with rugs and baskets and scratching posts and five-runged cat castles where cats of every color, texture, and size slept, roamed, washed themselves and each other, or crowded against the door, mewing, *Look! Someone's here. Maybe I can get petted.*

Not sure whether I was allowed in, I reached for the door handle. Ah-ha. Only someone with an I.Q. of 190 or, alternatively, very clever with levers could enter. Failures in both categories, Mom and I wistfully contemplated the cats through the closed door until a woman pushing a cart with water, detergent, and bags of clean and used litter smiled and asked, "You want in?"

I nodded, and she opened the door. Pulling on Mom's sleeve, I murmured, "Let's go."

Mom studied the linoleum. "I'll wait here. Pet the orange ones for me."

Then I realized it. I might be in heaven, but I was the only one there. "Mom? What's going on?"

"I'm fine," she insisted, though she obviously wasn't.

Mom taught me to love cats, to treat them not like people but intimate friends. She'd insisted that it's silly to think you can't talk to cats or understand them.

Now, the woman who had taught me all this treated the cats like a bunch of silent creatures. Scary creatures.

"You go," she repeated.

So I did. I even mastered the skill of opening the door—failure in front of so many judgmental felines felt too embarrassing. But in each room every orange cat I petted said, *No. Thanks for asking, but I'm fine where I am.*

Mom could tell from my face what they'd said.

Outside the third room, the volunteer caught up to us. "Were you looking for an older cat?"

"Not at all," we answered almost simultaneously. Then Mom smiled, finally, then she asked, "Why?"

"Because you keep going in the rooms where the older cats are."

So that's why they declined petting, playing, and even conversation.

"Tell me what you're looking for," the volunteer suggested. "Maybe I can help?"

Mom explained that she wanted a slender cat—so it wouldn't be too heavy to lift—with a pretty face. Orange would be good, but it couldn't look exactly like her poor Genji. That would hurt too much.

After several tries, Susan offered Mom a kitty named Akhiban. We settled on the sofa so they could get acquainted. Unfortunately, Akhiban fell instantly in love with me and wasn't subtle about his infatuation. Mom noticed. What I noticed was that Mom hadn't fallen for him. "I don't like his name," she admitted.

"Name him anything you want. Don't you think he's gorgeous?"

"He's okay. Genji was prettier."

In truth, Genji wasn't, but cat love, like every other kind, is in the eye of the beholder.

So Susan got back to cat shopping for Mom. Susan started with orange cats. Apparently, these are disproportionately male, which equals disproportionately large. Mom needed a cat she could easily slide into its carryall for vet trips.

Susan advanced from orange cats to smaller females. Quite a few of them joined us on the couch. But Mom complained that the black eyes of a mostly white one looked dirty. The Siamese was too old, and a gray one had a nicked ear. Every time a cat seemed perfect, it was part of a pair that couldn't be split up. Understandably, the staff made no exceptions to that rule. Mom didn't think she could handle two, not at her age. Then it was closing time and they wanted us out of there.

Determined to learn from the various setbacks, we returned right after lunch the following day. We could get Mom a cat. We knew it.

First we went to see Akhiban. This time he didn't like either of us but provided no information why.

As the hours passed, Mom's standards slipped lower and lower. The cat just had to be pretty—not gorgeous and certainly not necessarily orange. If it liked her okay and didn't weigh too much, she'd take it. That's what she said. Was that true, though?

Something else was going on, and I hadn't figured it out. Maybe the various cats I cuddled or jingled my car keys for knew the answer, but they weren't saying.

Susan was off today, so Karen, who was less patient, helped us. Like me, she seemed unsure that Mom really wanted a cat. "She's seen a lot of them," Karen whispered. "Is she serious?"

"My mother hasn't found the right one. Now she's interested in Akhiban again, but he was so unfriendly."

Mom, who'd wandered down the corridor by herself, returned in time to hear Karen explain, "Oh, that's not the same cat. They took Akhiban upstairs to rest, because you spent so much time with him. I guess they didn't bring him back."

I was about to ask whether Karen could get us the real Akhiban, but Mom interrupted. "No."

"You don't want Akhiban?"

Mom turned away from Karen, who realized that we needed a moment of privacy and disappeared. I guess working with all those cats taught Karen a thing or two about listening with your eyes.

There in the Humane Society, in a long corridor of cage after cage of cats scratching at the doors, begging us to notice them, to choose them, to love them, I folded my mother into my arms. She was careful not to make a sound, but I knew she was crying. She'd lost her husband. She'd lost the cat who'd kept her company and filled the empty bed a little bit after his absence. And her daughter lived a thousand miles away. Mom wept because, like all those caged cats, she couldn't have what she wanted.

I rocked her as we stood there, thinking about the gift and the horror of this place. Some cats were here because people had abandoned them. Others hissed or spit; both Susan and Karen had noted those. Several had the loveliest markings, came in the pearliest shades of gray. They would live out their lives here without starvation or euthanasia. There was that.

But except for curling up into a ball, sleeping too much, declining to eat, or driving off every connection, their choices weren't their own. Just like Mom.

"You know what?" I stooped so we could look into each other's eyes. "There's no hurry. It's not that you don't want a cat." I watched her exhale with relief, realizing that I'd unearthed the secret. "The cat you're supposed to have will find you. The way Genji did."

I took my hand off Mom's shoulder to scratch the forehead of an orange-and-white kitten. The little guy reached out both paws and cupped my fingers, tight. Satisfied with the capture, he purred, loud and secure.

Mom and I were both seeing Genji and his brothers and sisters crawling up the sides of the carton where some person, hoping for the best, had left them outside my dad's store all those years ago. Genji captured my Mom's hand and heart that day, and he held them still. I could see her watching the cat and not wanting any other paws on her arm, not now, not yet, not any more than she'd want a man other than my dad resting his cheek against hers.

A cat would choose Mom. She had to wait for that. However long it took, well, that would be just long enough.

—*Laurel Yourke*

Max, the "Stupid" Cat

"Here, kitty. Here kitty-kitty," I beckoned in the sweetest cat-calling voice I could muster. Like always, Max ran inside, grateful to get out of the pouring rain, but then promptly ran to another door to go back outside.

"He's so dumb," laughed my husband, Jim. "He doesn't know how to stay out of the rain. We should have named him 'Stupid Cat' instead of Max."

Neither of us knew much about cats, and we couldn't understand people who acted like their cats were their children. We'd had three cats, but they certainly weren't like members of the family.

Our children were excited over our first cat, the tiny orange ball of fur we kept only a month. He scratched the kids, and our son Clay was highly allergic to him.

Twenty years later, our second cat arrived one day. A pitiful-looking gray cat that wound itself around our legs while we sat on our deck, she looked hungry, so we fed her milk. We continued this, and, before long, she would walk to our refrigerator and meow "milk." Though we never took Kate to the vet or brushed or petted her much, Kate was content with food, water, and a warm place to sleep. She kept away mice and snakes. We had a great symbiotic relationship, but nothing more.

Our third cat showed up a few years after Kate. I told Clay, "You can keep her, but she's your responsibility." I never paid enough attention to Allie to judge whether or not she was smart. When Clay joined the Marines, I decided one cat was quite enough and took Allie to the pound, assuming the shelter would find her a good home.

My children and granddaughter, Amber, rode with me. The kids called me "cat killer" the whole way.

"Can you say 'felinicide'?" my son quipped.

Amber mimicked, "Fe-lin-i-cide." That toddler is now twenty-one, and I'm still not sure whether she's forgiven me for taking Allie to the pound.

Kate kept at her mouser job for years before she began to lose weight. She never appeared to be in pain, but one day she vanished. I was shocked to find I missed her, but I never felt guilty about our lack of time with her.

When a friend of our daughter, Melissa, had to move and find a home for her "inside cat who loved to be outside," we were happy to adopt a new mouser. His old owner arrived with as much paraphernalia as a newborn baby: two crystal bowls, a litter box, litter, a small carrier, and health records. She also left his brushes, after demonstrating how he loved to be petted and groomed. She discussed his daily schedule and the special food he preferred. She left a generous supply, along with his favorite treats.

Nervous as a new mom, I tried brushing and petting him, but I was afraid he'd bite. Max wandered around sniffing and exploring the house and didn't mess up anything. He used his litter box, ate, slept, and never seemed to miss his owner.

We gradually introduced him to the outside, making sure he stayed nearby. Max would meander a while, then come right back inside to eat or use the litter box. We gradually increased his time outdoors and moved the litter box into the garage. That's when we first realized we'd adopted a stupid cat.

We installed a kitty door in the garage. Max just looked at it, even when we tried coaxing him in with food. Jim also rigged up a small box equipped with a heat light, so Max wouldn't get too cold. Though he loved the garage, he refused to enter it except through our kitchen.

"I don't want to be tied down," I complained. "I want to be able to leave for a few days without having someone cat-sit."

When grandchildren visited, I asked them to try to train Max to use his cat door. One grandchild stood inside the garage and poked food through the opening, letting Max sniff it, while the other child stayed outside and fairly pushed him through the kitty door. After hours, he finally learned how to get where food, water, a litter box, and warmth waited.

Despite having mastered the cat door in the garage, Max continued to do the most awful things, like stalking birds and leaving them, dead, at our door. Once, when I opened the kitchen door, Max waltzed in with a live chipmunk in his mouth. I screamed, and he let go. We had an indoor chipmunk, alive, for days.

"Stupid cat," I said. "What's wrong with him? He has food!"

When we'd leave for several days, he wouldn't touch his food or water, and we'd return to see a dead something at our kitchen door.

"Max!" I'd scream. "What's wrong with you? You're so stupid. You have food you won't eat, and you drink from the birdbath when you have clean water."

So it went for years. Occasionally, we'd let Max inside when it was frigid, but basically he followed in

Kate and Allie's footsteps, staying outside except during harsh weather. I brushed and petted him occasionally. Max seemed to prefer it that way. He also would meet our cars every afternoon, but when we'd say, "Hello, Max," the silly cat would wander away, head held high, like he didn't know who we were.

Although he got in terrible fights, we never thought about taking him to a vet, not even for shots. We still felt he was just a mouser cat, a duty he did well.

Then came the year when life, as I had known it, ended. I developed chronic illnesses and had surgery and complications that left me in terrible pain twenty-four hours a day. I was so weak I couldn't walk to the mailbox and felt like I'd become an old woman overnight. That first winter on disability was quiet and lonely.

As I sat, miserably glued to my recliner, Max would come to the back door and meow. I'd let him in, he'd wander around and then settle down at my feet, totally content.

As I spent more time with him, I noticed he seemed to move slower in the morning. "Do your joints hurt, Maxie?" I asked one day.

Jim was amused at my new interest in Max, but he did research on cat years. "He's older than we are," Jim said.

I was shocked and recognized Max was often hurting too. I spent more time with him, brushing him daily. "Good therapy," I said, a bit embarrassed.

Before long, Max—who was becoming quite smart—would quietly curl up beside me, purring softly, as I slept. He never clawed the furniture, jumped on anything other than my lap, or had an accident. Soon, a food and water bowl also appeared in our kitchen. Max "told" us when he wanted out, which was fairly often, and it was sort of lonesome without him.

One day, as I talked to him, he put his paws on my chest, looked me in the eyes, and twisted his neck as if to say, *Stroke my head.* He butted it against my head and continued this until he taught me to stroke him under his chin and to butt my head against his.

Max was more sensitive to my moods and pains than many of my family and friends. When I felt most forlorn, he would quietly curl up beside me, his purring seemingly synchronized to my beating heart. *This is one amazing cat,* I thought.

One night my husband and I went to Starbucks at Barnes and Noble. While we sipped coffee we browsed several books, including one about cats. We bought it to continue reading at home. Suddenly, a lot of things Max had tried to tell us made sense. The more we read, the more we understood our sweet—and oh so smart—cat.

Soon I discovered he was petrified of storms. *Just like me,* I empathized.

As I listened and watched him, more understanding took place. His different meows each meant something. I'd praise him, "Maxie, what a smart boy you are!"

He still loved being outside, but one day I noticed him limping and saw white fur near the door. Max had a scratch over one eye. "Oh no, he got into another fight," I told Jim.

My husband assured me that Max would be okay, but he wasn't. He stayed inside and began hiding under our bed. We moved his food and water nearby, but he wouldn't eat. After a few days, Max allowed his ignorant parents to hold him. I gasped! His right front paw was swollen four times its normal size.

"How could we have been so stupid?" I wailed.

Panicked, I called my daughter, who has three large dogs. Her roommate has four cats. They both always have huge vet bills. I'd always thought doctors are for people, but now I realized they are for pets, too. I had no idea whom to call or how I'd get Max into the crate he'd outgrown. Most of all, I was terribly ashamed he'd had no shots in ten years.

"You've got to get him to our vet immediately," Melissa said. "I have to work, but Cat can come take you."

Swallowing my pride, I let her appropriately named roommate get Max into the large crate she brought.

I was fearful of a huge bill we couldn't afford, since my medical bills were still enormous. There was no money for emergencies like this, but I didn't care. I just wanted Maxie to live, and I prayed to have another chance to show him how much I loved him.

"The infection is really advanced. I'm not sure we can save him," the vet said.

After two days, Max did come home. My daughter's friend came every day to give him his medications. She knew exactly how to get him to open his mouth. We were amazed! When Jim and I took over giving his meds, it took both of us to get a few drops in his mouth.

The saddest thing was how passive our independent Max had become. Though weak, he preferred going outside to using his litter box. When he wanted out, he'd look at the door, and Jim would gently pick him up and place him a few feet into the yard. Max wouldn't move from that spot. He'd feebly try to bury his waste and then patiently wait to be picked back up.

In two weeks Max had enough energy to stay outside for few minutes, and a week after that, he decided he's been inside quite long enough, thank you. We were like two nervous, overprotective parents sending their only child off to school the first day. "What if that black cat bothers him again?" we fretted.

These days, I think we need Max more than he needs us. We have the mouser cat we trained, so Max only wants in when it's really hot or cold or during a storm. He wants to be petted when he's good and ready, and he loves being brushed, but most of the time the great outdoors, rather than with us, is where he prefers to be.

Max, our brilliant cat, struts down his sidewalk like the king of the world. He looks at us rather smugly. I can almost hear him meow to the next-door cat, *Thank goodness, I finally got my humans trained. They were so stupid I thought they'd never catch on. Now maybe I can enjoy my retirement days with a little peace!*

—*Elaine Young McGuire*

One Creature Great and Small

One icy morning, John, the garbage collector, found a scrawny kitten nearly frozen to death between a cardboard box and a trashcan. Several times over the last few weeks, John had seen a mother cat and several kitties in the neighborhood. The previous day, though, he saw the mother cat's body in the street, apparently hit by a car. A couple of babies from her litter hovered around, but zipped out of sight as soon as the truck banged its way toward the alley.

The day John spied the wad of icy fur beside the garbage can, subzero wind blasted snow in his face. John had just assumed the kitten was dead when it stirred; the tiny mouth opened and then one eye. John jerked off his warm, red plaid scarf, wrapped the cat into it, jumped into his truck, and kicked it into gear.

He looked at his watch. The animal clinic should be open by now, and it was only a few blocks away. When the garbage truck rattled to a stop in the nearly vacant parking lot, John still held the kitten, wrapped in the scarf, in his gloved hand. He hopped out of the truck, raced to the door, and tried the door with his remaining hand. It was locked.

Beating the door with his big fist, John yelled, "I've got a frozen animal here!"

Finally, he heard footsteps inside. As soon as the door swung open, John plowed through. "I found this kitty in an alley. I think he's about dead," John said, a lump forming in his throat.

The commotion brought Doc Winthrop to the waiting room. "What do you have there, John?" he asked.

"A kitty. He's a little feller. I think the cold's about got him."

"Well, bring him in," Doc said, reaching for the small plaid bundle in John's outstretched hand.

"I have to go finish my route, but I'll be back to pay for any care you give him," John said. A good feeling pulsed through him, knowing he'd done what he could and that Doc would do his best to help the cat.

That afternoon John returned to the animal hospital. "The kitten is still with us," Doc Winthrop said with a grin. "You sure he's a stray?"

"Yes. His mother was pretty wild, and I'd mentioned her to some of the homeowners I talked to in the neighborhood. They were mad because she kept having babies. I think they were considering putting them all in a gunnysack and dropping them into the river."

"Well, don't worry about the cost of care," the vet said. "You did your part in trying to save him. I'm doing my part. Maybe he'll make it."

The doc and his veterinary assistants muscled their expertise and energy into healing the tiny kitten, and he was a fighter. He made it through an hour-long surgery to remove more than half his severely frostbitten tail and part of a foot. He struggled to survive.

John checked on the little creature every day. It didn't take long before the growing ball of fur had made the animal clinic his kingdom. Half Pint, as the doc and his staff affectionately named him, was content to curl up on his perch near the front door most of the time, ignoring much of the clamor of the office. It took more than the usual dog's bark, pot-bellied pig's grunt, or parrot's squawk to interrupt his dreams.

Several times a day, though, Half Pint would stretch, make like he was going to sleep again, but then jump to the floor and saunter away toward the kennels. There, he would stroll the aisle between the caged dogs, who barked, bared their teeth, growled, and groaned their threats. The brave kitty didn't give a single one of them a glance. Like a satiated king of beasts taking a leisurely walk in the forest while tropical birds, monkeys, and squirrels screamed warnings, Half Pint, with what was left of his tail pointed high, would trot straight ahead as if the dogs weren't even there.

Once he had healed, the little cat with the big attitude had a much more important role in the clinic than just lounging and pumping up the canines' blood pressure. Half Pint became the official resident blood donor for injured and ill felines who needed a transfusion. His blood gave life to show breeds such as the Persian with the snowy, flowing coat, pansy-like face, and wall full of Grand Champion ribbons at home. His blood pulsed through a rotund Garfield look-alike and through myriad other scrawny cats suffering from accidents and disease.

Half Pint even saved a much-loved tabby whose tearful elderly owner had brought her to the clinic to be put to sleep. The tabby's foot had been partially amputated in a freak accident with a hamster cage. After seeing Half Pint strut through the animal hospital with his deformities and hearing his story, she decided to try to keep her cat alive and asked the doc to operate. Half Pint not only provided the blood for the surgery, he also provided the inspiration to do the surgery.

The kitten who started life as a scruffy half pint became a fifty-gallon asset to the clinic. When the veterinarian introduced me to him, I had never been a cat lover, had never had a pet as a child, and had children who were allergic to animals. Half Pint changed the way I thought about pets, and I've never forgotten him. What's more, I learned an important life lesson in courage and compassion from that back-alley kitty whose lowly heritage and deformed body didn't stop him from enjoying life and from becoming a hero.

As the old Christian hymn proclaims, "All creatures great and small / . . . the Lord God made them all."* Half Pint was one of the great ones.

—Ada Nicholson Brownell

"All Things Bright and Beautiful," lyrics by Cecil F. Alexander, 1848.

Nobody Gets Left Behind

I remember my first sighting of a Himalayan cat. I was about eight years old, and we had stopped for ice cream one Sunday afternoon. All of the shops near the ice cream parlor were closed, and it was mere chance that I happened to spot the sleeping pile of fur in one of the closed shop's windows. It slowly opened its eyes, and I marveled at the flatness of its face and the odd mix of size, fur, and lethargy. I later learned that this cat had the run of the place but tended to prefer sleeping in the window to running around. Cat sightings became an added perk to the already highly anticipated ice-cream stops.

When I moved into my own apartment and could choose whatever pet I wanted, it didn't take long for me to decide upon a Himalayan. Margot was better than a roommate; she listened to my troubles and asked for very little in the way of care. She loved to be held. My friends called her "Liquid Kitty" because she fit the shape of her container—which happened to be my arms. Her only annoying habit, sleeping on my pillow just above my head, even became endearing with time.

Margot ("Marg," by then) moved apartments with me a few times, never complaining. When I traveled, I frequently plunked down an additional $150 to give her the right to ride under the seat in front of me. Happy as long as she was with me, she accompanied me wherever and whenever I went. When I got married, my husband knew that merely accepting my cat was unacceptable, that she must be loved.

Marg was my best little sidekick until my daughter was born, which, as it naturally would, changed the way we were. People loved to tell me old wives' tales about cats and babies, mocking me about my other, furry baby. Marg retreated into the background slowly, always remaining a respectful distance away from the baby. As time went by, the distance became larger and larger, and I saw less and less of her.

One day, I realized that I hadn't seen Marg in a while. She had taken to hiding in the closet and under beds, so I didn't think much of it. A day went by, though, and I became more worried, actively searching her favorite nooks and crannies. Another day went by, and I enlisted my husband to search the attic, storage areas, everywhere. He proclaimed her missing, but I still didn't believe.

I never let my cat outside. I was always very attentive to the door to protect her from her own nomadic urges, not to mention our busy street. I remembered, finally, a trip outside to take out the garbage, when I maybe, just maybe, had left the door cracked. It seemed I had forgotten to take care of my old friend in my distraction from taking care of the new love of my life.

I made a few lost-cat flyers, still not believing Marg was really gone, and hung them in all the obvious places. A few more days went by, and it finally hit me that my cat had run away. I was totally despondent, exhausted from taking care of a newborn, and beside myself with guilt and sadness for having neglected my loyal companion.

I made a few more flyers, 800 to be exact. I put the baby in the stroller and handed them out door-to-door to the entire neighborhood. It rained. I took the car and continued, a little more slowly. It froze. Eventually, I accepted reality and made a trip to the animal shelter. As I filled out the "lost cat" form, I sadly checked "none" when it came to the part asking about identification and collar.

The woman behind the counter said, "Put a tag on your next cat."

"I'm not getting another cat!" I shrieked. Then I burst into tears.

I had all but given up hope. My husband and friends thought I was insane, with all the flyers and drive-arounds. After two weeks of bad weather, the sun came out. I put on my running clothes and shouted to my husband that I was going for a jog. Then I grabbed my tape gun and my last few flyers. One more try.

After hanging the last of the flyers, I slowly headed back home, defeated. As I came up the walk, I saw her. Margot! She was sitting in the driveway, looking sad and suspicious. I approached slowly, and she hesitated for only a moment before letting me gather her up, skin and bones, and carry her inside.

After that day, she was all purrs and affection, preferring to share the attention than to rough it on her own. I tried to be more attentive to her, too, and less seemed to be enough for her. Years went by, and along the way Marg took up residence in my daughter's room. I don't know another cat that would let a toddler hold her with such patience.

About a year ago, we found out we would be moving to France. There were a million things to do—sell our home, sell our cars, pack up a household worth of stuff, sell and store things we didn't need, say good-bye to family and friends. To make matters more complicated, I was pregnant again. With all this to deal with, my primary worry was how to take my cat with us.

I discussed the medical certificate with our vet and the procedure with the airline. Her ticket would cost as much as ours, and she would not be allowed to ride under my seat like before. My husband grumbled (jokingly) that we should just buy a new cat with all that money. As if there were another Margot to buy.

We were down to the last week, and I discovered that the microchip I'd had implanted in Marg after the running-away episode might not be sufficient identification to import her to France. I called the manufacturer in tears and begged them to rush-ship a new one. I went to the FDA with my paperwork. It was incomplete without the new chip information. Back to the vet, back to the FDA. I hoped that it would be enough to secure her entry into the country.

I wondered if I was putting my cat—and certainly, my family—through too much. We were moving a family of four, and I was running around all over the city with paperwork for my cat. One day my daughter asked me if Margot was coming with us. I mumbled yes, hoping it was true. Then she said something that struck a nerve: "In a family, nobody gets left behind." She was right, of course.

The flight went well, the paperwork was sufficient, and when we arrived, my cat was waiting for us on the other side. Despite the long trip in the back of the plane, Margot looked cheerful and well cared for. Like always, she adjusted to her new surroundings quickly.

Now that she is here, she continues to watch over us all. When my daughter was adjusting to the language barrier and a new preschool, Margot stood sentry by her bed at night, watching over her and ready to dry tears with a furry cuddle and a purr. She slips into my son's room at night, too—not to suck the breath of life out of him in the middle of the night, but to jump to attention should he wake. And for me, she simply waits for a call and runs to be picked up and held.

As a matter of fact, she's next to me right now, and as soon as I type my last word, I will carry her upstairs with me, where she will sleep on my pillow and warm my head, like always.

—*Amanda Callendrier*

One of a Kind

I'd always sensed something was not quite normal about my cat, Amadeus. There were hints from the start—like the way he did nothing but hide under furniture and hiss the first few days after my husband, Ron, brought him home. I'd never had a cat before, so I was at a loss. I tried coaxing him out with toys, with milk, with tuna. Nothing worked. This strange specimen came with no instruction manual, and none of the books on cat care seemed to apply to him. Page after page featured adorable kittens batting at strings and showing off their fat fuzzy tummies, but nothing resembling my hiding, hissing kitten. Convinced the little beast was possessed or defective, I was ready to send him back to the breeder. Then Ron informed me the hissing was all for show.

"Just reach in there and pet him," he said. "He won't bite."

Slowly, cautiously, I reached my hand under the bulky antique dresser that was the current lair of the psycho-kitty. As my hand moved closer, the hissing grew louder, like I'd kicked a nest of vipers. Amadeus backed himself as far into the corner as he could and bared his pointy little teeth. I risked one finger and scratched him under the chin.

The hissing stopped, and Amadeus froze. I scratched a little more. The fierce teeth disappeared into an expression that resembled confusion. A little more scratching, and his neck stretched forward. Longer and longer it grew as I gradually withdrew my hand. Finally, he took a step forward.

In no time, we were best buddies. But he did not suddenly become normal. Oh, no. New signs of "not normal" emerged almost daily. For one thing, Amadeus developed a love of ambush. I would walk innocently down the hallway, my mind on a million things, when suddenly from a doorway a fuzzy gray blur would streak out, ricochet off my thigh, and blast away to safety. A few times, I'm pretty sure I heard him laughing as he disappeared.

Then there were the monsters. My cat was convinced our home was infested with them. When I made the bed, there were sheet monsters. Amadeus would scramble across the bottom sheet, his eyes as big as headlights and his whiskers at attention, swiping at the menacing pockets of air. Then I'd throw the top sheet over him, and he'd flip over to claw frantically at the monsters descending from above. Smaller but trickier mutations of the bed monsters were the sock monsters. When I lounged around the house in socks and no shoes, Amadeus attacked my toes, for where there was motion, there were monsters. When I wrote, there were paper monsters. The nearer my deadlines loomed, the more monsters Amadeus would spot in my precisely arranged and precariously teetering stacks of papers. He'd flail through them, front paws waving at the speed of light, back paws propelling him through the flurry of pages like a bullet train through a snow drift. He left no monster unturned . . . and no paper uncrumpled, untorn, or unslobbered-on. These minor sacrifices were of no concern to Amadeus. His devotion to monster hunting was unstoppable.

Each time Amadeus would spring some new version of "not normal" on me, I'd report it to my husband. "He's not normal," I'd say.

Ron would just shake his head. "He's *your* cat."

To which I'd counter, "Yeah, but you picked him."

In the end, Ron always leapt to Amadeus's defense. "His father used to run into walls," he'd explain with admiration in his voice, even pride.

"Is that supposed to reassure me?" I'd ask. It occurred to me that my cat might not be the only one who wasn't normal, but that's another story.

Yes, I noticed many clues that Amadeus was not normal. But it was the special way he woke us one fateful night that gave me all the proof I needed.

I was sleeping peacefully enough to make the dead whine with envy when a strange sound dragged me toward consciousness. It was a rasping, high-pitched shriek that came in quick bursts: *Scree! Scree! Scree!* Closer it came, closer. Then I felt Amadeus jump up onto the bed, and my imagination kicked into warp speed. *What was wrong? Was he injured? Choking?*

I reached over, flipped on the lamp, and slipped on my glasses. There before my squinting, blinking, sleep-blurry eyes stood Amadeus—with a bat's head clamped between his teeth and the rest of the bat sticking out of his mouth, squirming and flapping like there was no tomorrow. The bat's fear for its future was the most logical part of the whole scene. I gave a suitably logical response: I screamed.

Satisfied he had my attention, Amadeus proceeded to oh-so-matter-of-factly spit the bat out onto my feet—*pa-tooey*. My eternal thanks went out to the inventor of blankets, because those were all that separated my skin from the now-free and logically unhappy bat.

Luckily for me, the bat was a bit disoriented. It flapped and flopped around on the bed, shrieking the whole time. Meanwhile, Amadeus sat himself down and gave me one of those classic cat looks. You know the type. This one said, *What a lucky woman you are. Just think, you could belong to a lesser cat, some ordinary cat. But no, you're with me. See what I've done for you this time? I brought you a toy that is also a snack. Or maybe it's a snack that's also a toy. Doesn't matter. I brought it just for you. And it's only slightly used. Because that's what a great cat I am. You lucky, lucky woman. You may shower me with gratitude and adoration now. I'll take a side of tuna with that.*

Right. I jumped out from under those covers, yelling something to the effect of "Get that thing out of here!"

Ron got up, mumbling something that sounded like a darker version of "He's your cat."

This gave the bat just enough time to get its bearings and make a break for it. It flew in unsteady circles, barely missing the ceiling fan.

Amadeus's eyes turned into glow-in-the-dark saucers. He crouched low, saucers tracking the only slightly used toy-snack, waggled his butt a few times, and then launched himself at the fluttering, shrieking bundle of fun. He clipped the bat with his paws, sending it spiraling toward the ground, but the thing was resilient. It righted itself and flew out the open bedroom door and down the hallway with Amadeus in hot pursuit.

Our pursuit was not nearly so hot. By the time we reached the living room, the bat was cruising just below ceiling altitude. Amadeus watched it, dancing from one paw to the other. Now his expression said, *Look! It's a mouse! And it's a bird! It's a mouse-bird!* He then demonstrated the proper operating procedures for a mouse-bird. He crouched low, waggled his butt, and launched himself into the air. This time he snatched the mouse-bird out of the air and pulled it to the floor. Clutching the mouse-bird's head gently but firmly between his teeth, he high-stepped out of sight with his prize. I can't be positive, but it sounded like he finished with an end-zone dance.

After a quick huddle for a game plan, Ron and I split up to scavenge a bat-sized box and a piece of cardboard. We took them into the bedroom. There was Amadeus, playing with his mouse-bird toy-snack.

"You're not normal," I told him.

He blinked once and hit me with a look that said, *You're talking to a cat and imagining a reply. Who's not normal?*

"Point taken," I replied.

Ron dropped the box over the bat, trapping it. Then I carefully slid the cardboard underneath.

Amadeus gave me a new look: *Hey. I'm not finished with that.*

Ron took the bat out to the backyard and set it free.

Back inside, Amadeus's look now said, *What the %&#$ did you do with my mouse-bird toy-snack?* "You know," I said to him, "other cats bring their people ordinary mice and plain old birds. Often prekilled. Why would you need to bring a mouse-bird, I mean, a bat? A live one?"

Amadeus did not reply. He could be mysterious like that when the mood struck him.

No, Amadeus was definitely not normal. Yet, he was a great, true friend. There was a whole world of personality—maybe multiple personalities—in that little package. So when, after seventeen years and eleven months, his health failed and we had to let him go, we were crushed. So crushed we decided not to get another cat right away. It just didn't seem right.

Now, a year later, we're ready to bring home another cat. We know no cat can take Amadeus's place. We don't expect to find another one like him. That's why just to make sure there's enough "not normal" to go around, we're bringing home two kittens.

—*Denise R. Graham*

A Cat Named Bob

Wind was howling its raucous song, noisy verses gathered from Canadian prairies, down across the Dakotas and Kansas. The cacophony swept across Oklahoma's panhandle like a million coyotes in chorus. The year was 1935, and I was four years old.

During the spring in that wide open country, it was rare to have a day without wind. When it gathered strength in its unchecked journey across thousands of miles, the wind sounds could be frightening to a small child.

On one such morning, I lay tucked snugly in my low bed, wriggling deeper into a cocoon of wool comforters made by my grandmother. The front door opened with a thump, wind driving it hard against the wall as Dad came in. Before dawn, when I'd wakened momentarily, I had heard him leave the house. Later, I would learn that he had "gone on a story" for the local newspaper. He had been invited to accompany the town marshal to check on an old man who lived in a sod house far out of the little town where we lived.

Mama and Dad's voices were low murmurs as they tried not to wake me that morning. They often spoke that way, for we lived in two rooms of a large frame house that had been divided into small apartments. My iron bed was in a corner of the front room, which also served as the kitchen, dining, and living rooms. I liked lying in my bed listening to Mama and Dad talk, although often I did not understand the words. I closed my eyes and dozed again. When next I opened them, I found myself staring into cat eyes just a few inches away. Through my sleepiness, a whole cat face emerged. I could not see its body, as its chin rested on the edge of my bed.

Cats were always a part of my young life, tabbies, mostly, that I loved and cuddled. Gradually, as I came fully awake, I realized that the cat now so close to my face was different. After the yellow eyes, what I noticed most was its alert, pointed ears with little tufts of fur standing up at the tips like tiny flags. Tiger stripes patterned its head and face. The cat continued to gaze into my eyes, as if we were in a contest to see which of us could last the longest without blinking. The mouth opened widely in a yawn, revealing efficient feline teeth and a bright pink tongue. Then the head disappeared as the cat curled up on the braided rug next to my bed.

I sat up then to view the whole creature, deciding immediately that this must be a present from Dad to me. Dad's gifts were always different, never just a doll or book. I looked down and saw that while the head had stripes, the cat's body had spots, and it was the largest cat I had ever seen! In fact, this cat appeared to be almost as large as I.

Mama came over when she saw that I was awake and cautioned me not to pet the cat until it knew us better. At breakfast, Dad told me about the old man who had raised the cat after it was orphaned while still a tiny kitten. He said the man had been a "hermit," and I had to have that word explained. The old man had died, and Dad feared the big cat would die if left on its own.

"It's a bobcat," Dad told me.

I knew there were men named Bob and assumed he just meant that this cat was called Bob. So Bob he was.

As with the domestic cats we had had, I quickly bonded with Bob. Mama was afraid to let him outdoors in case he got lost in town. Bob had been accustomed to roaming outside at night in the country and sleeping on the old man's bed during the day. In our small apartment at night, Bob paced back and forth, his claws clicking on the linoleum floor. As he walked, he yowled and howled. Eventually, he would settle down at the foot of my bed, but Mama complained of being kept awake for hours by Bob's nocturnal restlessness.

What Bob liked best was sitting with me in Dad's big rocking chair. Bob was so big that he almost covered me when he tried to lie on my lap. His tail and back legs would hang off on one side and his head would loll halfway off the chair on the other, but he took long naps, purring loudly in his sleep. I loved it when he slept like that, for it gave me a chance to explore the intricate patterns of his fur. If I touched his whiskers, his hind feet gave a little kick, which I found funny. And I loved his big squishy paws, so enormous compared to those of other cats I had known.

Bob's wildness showed strongly when he was hungry. A can of salmon cost ten cents in those days, and that was the usual fare for our cats. Bob quickly learned to recognize the sound of a can opener and rushed toward Mama every time he heard it. As the days passed, this rushing became more aggressive and a low growl came from Bob's throat. Mama grew convinced that he might attack her. He had already scratched her once when she did not get the salmon can open fast enough to suit him. He kept his claws sheathed with me, as if he knew I was a baby, but he sometimes played roughly with Dad.

Mom preferred for Dad to feed Bob and began dropping hints that he should be looking for another home for the big cat. He was expensive to feed on Dad's Depression-era salary. Things came to a head one afternoon when Dad was late getting home from work. As Mama started to open a can of salmon, Bob gathered his feet together as if he might jump on her. She hopped up on our dining table, forgetting that cats can jump to great heights and the table was no protection at all. There she stood, "treed," after hurling the half open can to the floor. Bob was struggling to extract his fish when Dad arrived. Of course, Dad laughed when he saw Mama up on the table, which did not help anything.

When I woke up the next morning, I looked all around for Bob, but he was gone. Dad had taken him to live on a ranch, and I never saw Bob again.

We had no money for film that year, so no pictures of Bob exist. But even now, I can lie in my bed on an early morning when the wind howls through the trees, turn my head on the pillow, and in my mind see two tufted ears above a pair of golden eyes peeping mysteriously over the edge of the mattress.

—*Marcia E. Brown*

The Only Good Cat
Dad Ever Met

"You got a what?" my dad said in disbelief. "I never met a cat that was worth a darn. Your Aunt Eileen used to bring cats home when we were kids. They were either climbing my mother's lace curtains or streaking through the house like wildfire, hissing and scratching when someone tried to touch them.

"I wouldn't have a cat in the house for anything," he continued. "I thought I'd taught you that dogs are the best pets. Dogs are always happy to see you, especially if you've had a really bad day; always ready to go fishing or hunting, take a walk, or just sleep at your feet. Shoulda got a dog, you'll see."

"You're probably right"—I grinned through the telephone—"but you know that Al and I both travel a few days a week, and it wouldn't be fair to leave a dog in a kennel half the time. Cats use the litter box and don't need to be let out at night. They eat the food you leave only when they're hungry, and they can easily be left alone for a few days," I felt obligated to explain. "And Dad, he's a purebred Himalayan. His long, fluffy white hair is tinged with orange at the ears and on his tail. He's very tiny and at only a hundred dollars, he's a bargain!"

"Only a hundred dollars! You actually paid money for a cat? Where did I go wrong?" I could see his eyes roll.

"You will learn to love him, I promise. We're going to bring him over to meet you."

"Don't hurry," he said only half-jokingly.

I needn't have worried. Prinz was adorable and intent on winning the affection of anyone who came into sight. I'm sure he sensed Dad's hesitation and immediately rallied to the challenge. It was all over within an hour. He circled Dad's recliner, sniffing his shoes in passing, and then went to sit across the room and watch him for a bit. Another round of the recliner, more sniffing, a few moments of eyeing Dad's lap, and Prinz was ready for the kill. He turned on his tiny body's loud purr machine, stared directly into Dad's eyes, jumped onto his lap, and settled in for a short nap.

Within minutes, Dad was gently stroking the cat and murmuring to him softly. But I distinctly heard him say, "Prinz, you're the best kitten I've ever met." At that, Prinz woke, stretched his body out to its full eight-inch length, and climbed up Dad's chest to nuzzle his face.

"Shoulda got a dog," I said with a smile.

"Nah, this cat likes me," he said sheepishly.

It didn't take long for them to become buddies. Soon Dad was making special toys for Prinz and bringing him treats. One day he showed up casually dragging a cluster of duck feathers from the tip of an old ice-fishing pole. Prinz feigned disinterest until Dad propped the pole against the stone fireplace wall with the feathers suspended just barely out of reach. He couldn't resist the urge to jump and leap and attack.

Prinz even taught Dad to play hide and seek! They'd chase each other around the house, then stop, hide around a corner, and try to scare each other. I swear Prinz would leap up in the air with all four paws stretched wide, his mouth fully open, and spit an abbreviated *mewrt* that mimicked Dad's "boo!"

It was good to hear Dad laugh. It had been several years since his prostate cancer diagnosis and treatment, and the disease had recently returned with a vengeance. Metastasized to bone, cancer takes its toll slowly and is incredibly painful. For the next few years Dad would live on heavy medication, sleep fitfully, and spend most of his time in the old recliner, while Prinz grew into a young adult, watched the changes, sensed the need to slow down, and remained a solid friend and willing lap companion for hours at a time.

During Dad's last few years, as our out-of-town demands increased, Al and I would often leave Prinz with "Grandpa and Grandma" for several days at a time. Dad found comfort in that small warm body with its loud, vibrating purr snuggling close at his side. We tried to talk him into a kitten of his own, but he refused, reminding us that Prinz was the only good cat he'd ever met.

A few weeks before Dad died, hospice delivered a hospital bed to the house, hoping the adjustable positions would ease the pain and relieve developing bedsores. Other equipment also arrived—a portable toilet chair to keep next to the bed, oxygen, and a walker, so he could walk to the kitchen or den when he felt up to it. The hospice nurses came twice a day. Al and I packed our bags along with the cat's food and litter box, suspended work obligations, and moved in with Mom and Dad to be close at hand and help with the necessary twenty-four-hour-a-day caretaking.

They say cats know when someone is dying. When Dad asked for Prinz one afternoon, we realized that we hadn't seen him yet that day. We searched the house, frantically looking under the beds and the furniture, inside the closets, and shining flashlights behind the furnace and all of the stuff stored in the basement. Prinz had always been an inside cat, never wanting to go outdoors, but we were sure he'd slipped out the previous afternoon when the oxygen tank had been delivered. We searched the neighborhood and, at Dad's insistence, tacked signs on telephone poles and put an ad in the local newspaper.

After a few days we gave up hoping for his return and began hoping that he had been found by someone who would give him a good, loving home. For the rest of us, losing the cat was painful, but it was secondary to the pain of knowing we were going to lose Dad soon. For Dad, losing the cat was a constant worry. That whole last week the entire family gathered and focused on helping Dad let go, talking about our oldest best memories, thanking him for countless little things he had done or said that had enriched our lives, and just holding his hand and telling him we loved him. As his mind and body weakened, he often slipped away from reality for brief periods of time. Then he would suddenly wake with a quietly commanding and yet serene composure to focus on us—to make sure we were at peace with his leaving and with each other. And several times a day, he'd ask if Prinz had come back yet.

By then, Dad couldn't sleep for more than twenty minutes at a time, and the rest of us took turns staying awake and accompanying him on his nightly time travels into dream, imagination, and memory. I can still feel his arm around my waist, on my first night shift, as we sat on the edge of his bed with the blanket wrapped around our shoulders and "felt" our feet warm to the glowing campfire he saw on the floor in front of us. We looked up from that cozy fire to feel the cool breeze across our fire-warmed faces as we counted the stars in the black night sky. We listened to the animals rustling in the woods and looked for eyes reflecting the light of the lantern hanging in the tree near the tent. The air smelled of smoke, lake, wet sand, and pine trees. It was a great night. I was once again his little girl, and he was my protector, my daddy.

On my next night shift, I "walked" with him though a sunny meadow. His description of our sun-tanned faces almost hidden under our old straw fishing hats may have been drawn from memory or from a vision into his new reality. It didn't matter to me. He told me how happy he was that I had walked with him to the edge of heaven, and he asked me to bend low and smell the sweetness of the beautiful flowers—like the sweet peas that grew thick and wild on the fence row along the path to the garden on his grandparents' farm. His voice grew quiet and serious. His eyes sharpened, and he cocked his head as if listening. "There are no airplanes here! Listen to the sound of the air," he said, almost in a whisper. "Only birds and butterflies fly here." I knew his mind had brought him back home when he added, "I have to remember to fill the bird feeders."

Then, just a few days before Dad took his last breath, we heard Mom's scream coming from the basement stairs. Prinz, as terrified as Mom, was sitting wide-eyed and trembling at the bottom of the steps. For an entire week he hadn't eaten, drunk any water, or used the litter box. He was thin and very tired. We sensed that he knew what time it was. He had hidden for a week, evidently to avoid what he just didn't want to deal with. But now, as if sensing the need, he had to come back to say good-bye.

I carried him up the stairs and put him in Dad's lap. Dad's eyes misted as he picked up the cat and held him to his face. "Prinz, you came back! I was so worried. I wanted to tell you that you are the best animal in the whole world. I missed you."

The rest of the day Prinz rarely left Dad's side, except to eat and spend a few minutes watching the birds from the kitchen window.

The next morning Dad woke from a short nap looking a little confused, struggled to focus, and then smiled. "I'm glad you're here," he said softly. "Listen.

I have something important to say. I've been to the river. It is beautiful. I've seen my mother standing on the other side, reaching out and waiting for me. Others were coming to gather behind her," he said, checking off names on his fingers: Grandma, Grandpa, uncles, aunts, friends, and a niece who had died as a child. He smiled again and said, "We all have to cross that river someday. I'm ready to go. It's going to be all right."

He asked that we be sure to fill his bird feeders. My brother poured seed up to the tops, and we watched the birds gather all day. Cardinals, sparrows, chickadees, and gold finches all flitted about together and chirped noisily, while Prinz sat on the stool and watched them through the kitchen window.

Dad died that afternoon, holding Mom's hand, his last breath leaving peacefully and with the love of the entire family surrounding him in his bed, our hands touching his face, his hair, his feet. After saying our final good-byes, we walked together back to the kitchen, looked out, and saw that the birds were gone. Prinz sat at the window with his eyes focused skyward. We like to think that the birds, too, felt his last breath rising and were providing escort services to heaven and that Prinz was remembering his friend, the man he had taught to love a cat.

—*Judy Swanson*

A Universal Language

No nouns. No verbs. No ideas. I checked the clock. My copy deadline for a classical CD hovered like a shadow behind me. I typed some exploratory phrases on baroque music, then turned and yanked open the window, ushering in a spring breeze that brushed the old linen drape against my arm. I deleted a string of broken words from the computer and shivered. Someone watched me as I worked.

I wheeled my chair around. Eyes of bronze stared through the open window. Intense as lasers, tiger eyes judged me, the writer, coming up empty.

"Going to report me to the client?" I reached to touch the thin, gray kitty on the windowsill. My gesture sent the tabby scuttling off toward the nearby alley.

This was the closest I'd come to the little cat. When I first noticed the skinny, feral animal prowling around, I started putting bowls of food by the garage.

Although he demolished the tuna nuggets, the wild creature scrambled off whenever I approached.

Today, though, I did not need the distraction of cats. Time was running short.

I touched the button on my tape player, and the "Hallelujah Chorus" from Handel's *Messiah* swept through my office/apartment, opening forgotten drawers of musical memory. The power of the piece stirred rich harmonics in my mind. Finally, like a harpsichord artist, my fingers flew over the computer keyboard. Taking a break, I rewound the tape and belted out the "Chorus" lyrics in gratitude to Handel's genius. To my surprise, the shy kitten leapt onto the window to listen. I put a saucer of food near the sill in appreciation of his attendance and read my copy aloud for his approval.

After that morning, the gray tabby came regularly to my window. Two weeks later, I once again sang a series of hallelujahs as I revised the same liner notes, and the cat scooted through the window to join me in my simple life. As rewrite assistant, his paws played across my computer keys. As critic, he snoozed in boredom over any tired literary devices. As editor, he studied the scripts I'd stashed in the closet and carefully rearranged the pages.

Scooter stayed busy, catching flies that stopped by uninvited or displaying the art of napping on any splash of sunshine that fell into the room. My feline companion especially liked to sniff fresh blossoms of day lilies.* Always, when I sang Handel's "Hallelujah Chorus," he'd jump to the desk, cocking his head and gazing into my eyes.

Through summer, autumn, and winter, the drapes trembled from zephyrs, drafts, and winds. And the kitten became a cat.

One day, after a long business conference, when I unlocked the apartment, no cat galloped to greet me. Instead, I found Scooter's still body sprawled on the floor under the desk. I picked up the limp animal and fled to the veterinary hospital, where he was rushed to emergency for examination.

The doctor's face was grim. "Your cat's in a deep coma. I can start an intravenous line and order tests, but . . ."

"Will he be okay?"

"Unfortunately, you'd better prepare for the worst. Should I continue treatment?"

The smell of antiseptic clouded my mind, but I nodded permission. On the way home I bought a bunch of lilies. At the desk I buried my face deep inside the bouquet, hoping the pollen memory would ease the thought of losing my dear tabby. I played cat music, but couldn't sing. I pushed up the window and set bands of halleluiahs free to float outside. Then I cried into the folds of the faded linen drapes.

The next morning at the hospital, I produced my battery-operated tape player. The receptionist led me to a room filled with pets on the mend. Scooter's still form lay splayed like an animal rug on the bottom of his cage.

"Condition unchanged. Sorry," said the attendant filling water bowls at the sink.

"I'd like to play Scooter his favorite song," I said.

"Your cat's a music lover?"

"He's partial to Handel. Whenever I play this piece and sing, he jumps on my desk and listens."

The attendant threw me a curious look.

"Honest." I stroked soft cat fur through the bars.

"Couldn't hurt." The attendant delivered fresh water to waiting patients. "But keep the sound down."

I pushed "play" and lowered the volume. The room quieted as music calmed the other animals. Through slow tears, I sang to my silent pet and watched for any sign of improvement, but Scooter's bronze eyes remained closed. He slept in a distant place even Handel couldn't reach.

The final notes sounded. "I have to leave for work. Would you mind playing the song for him now and then?"

"Actually, the music's a nice addition."

I called the hospital at noon.

"Nothing to report," the doctor said. "And the expected time for recovery is diminishing."

Late that afternoon I took the bouquet of lilies to the animal hospital. The attendant sat on a stool, writing notes on a clipboard.

I waved the lilies back and forth in front of Scooter's cage, sending a faint ribbon of fragrance to his pink bud nose. "His favorite flower."

The attendant looked up. "He has a preference?"

"He nestles his face in the petals."

"I see."

"Could I put the vase inside his room? It's plastic. Unbreakable."

The attendant came over to Scooter's cage. "Oh, heck, if the container spills, it's just water." He released the latch lock.

I propped the flowers in a corner of the enclosure. "We're like two souls, my cat and I, speaking a universal language in which flowers and music are the nouns and verbs connecting us."

"I see that. Good luck to you both."

Back at the office I struggled with a tight deadline, but the absence of one small cat crept like white sound from room to room. The presence of absence, like the din of silence, invaded the apartment, papered the ceilings and walls, and inserted itself between the pages of the old scripts in the closet. I put away my project. The night was long and sleepless.

When I arrived at the pet hospital the next morning, the attendant was waiting by the door. "Lady, lady, your cat is alive. He's awake. I played his song first thing, and now he's sniffing the lilies."

I rushed to my furry friend. "Scooter! Oh Scooter, welcome back to the world."

Halleluiahs swung through the air on timeless trapezes. The cat's faint purring made an obbligato to the joy of wakefulness, as tiger eyes gazed through me, serious, bronze, and present.

The veterinarian diagnosed diabetes and showed me how to administer shots to an irritated cat. "It's amazing the way he fought his way back."

"Why do you think he made it?" I asked.

"Veterinary science would say the medication kicked in," he said, smiling. "But I wouldn't discount the power of music and the scent of flowers."

Scooter came home to critique my writing and catch flies, to nap and nuzzle, and to listen to Handel. In our universal language—in songs of joy and in the fragrance of lilies—our conversations continue. Hallelujah. Hallelujah.

—*Connie Spittler*

*Day lilies and other types of lilies are poisonous to cats if ingested and can cause acute kidney damage.

Gangsta Tabby

Our vet gave us a daunting ultimatum. "His wounds are healing, but it's only a matter of time before Harry gets seriously injured. I strongly advise you to think about either keeping him in all the time or trying to find a home for him a long way from other cats, perhaps on a farm somewhere."

Harry is a beautifully marked tabby with the face of an angel and the mind of a thug. He does not like other cats; he does not like them anywhere near our house or garden. Since they no longer hung around our garden, Harry now tracked them down and fought them wherever he found them!

After an assortment of injuries to his legs and his stomach and having had both sides of his face opened and drained from fights in battle, we knew we had to face this dilemma. On one trip to the vet, they had to shave his paw to give him an injection, so they could operate on his face. Afterward, we kept him inside for a few days. The first time we let him out again, he returned with fresh scars on the shaved paw, and I ended up in tears!

With our other two cats, Rosie and Brandy, Harry was no problem at all. Rosie was only eighteen months when we'd brought Harry into the house from an animal shelter, and he regarded her partly as mum and partly as big sister. If he was unruly in the house, Rosie gave him a smack in the face with her paw as a warning. If this warning did not work, she waited her moment and then stood astride him, trapping him underneath her superior weight. This resulted in cries for help from Harry, until we rescued him or she decided to let him go.

We could never part with Harry, even though he was the cause of all the trouble in the house: locked in wardrobes, stuck in drawers, stealing food, leaping across the bed in the middle of the night because he wanted to wake us up so we could chase him. He was famous in the little lane we live in for two things. First, he wrecked our neighbor's louvered blinds in pursuit of their cat—in their house. They had left their door open one summer day, and Harry chased their cat inside and up into a bedroom. Our neighbor, Steve, walked in and heard the commotion, and Harry came flying downstairs, only to find Steve had closed the door behind him. Harry panicked and in the process ripped their blinds in an attempt to get out.

His second claim to fame involved Steve's daughter, Megan, when she was around five years old. She was walking along, trailing her rag doll behind her, when Harry decided to "go for it." He grabbed the doll out of her hand, took off over a fence with it in his mouth, and disappeared into some shrubs. Megan was distraught, and we all had to go and hunt for her doll, while Harry sat in the sun cleaning himself and looking at us as if we were nuts.

Many of his fights were with a nearby cat called Sylvester. Harry was going into *his* house and stealing *his* food!

We were apprehensive about being able to make a housecat of Harry. So was the vet. We knew it would require patience balanced with discipline. At first, we persuaded Harry from the door by picking him up and giving him a cuddle. He even got the odd tidbit if he saw the other two had got out and he was left inside.

Brandy had come to us as the lodger who stayed, and he went out a lot. Rosie was rather timid outside and generally only went out for five minutes or so so we started to keep her in more if Harry was in view, so as to limit the amount of time he was left in the house. We only let Rosie out when Harry was busy or looking out a window.

Harry has always been a window-oriented cat, rather than a hearth cat. Now, he spent every moment at different windows of the house. At times, we felt sorry for him, sitting at the back door waiting to be let out or at an open window, sniffing the fresh air. Whenever a cat wandered into our garden, Harry would stand on his back legs, hissing and howling. This was a good reminder to us that if he were outside, he would be fighting with them.

It took nine months, but he mainly accepted that he did not get out. There are times even yet, some three years later, when he still howls at the front door.

No one, least of all us, likes to deprive a cat of his freedom, and it hasn't been easy. We are convinced, however, that this is the only way we could stop Harry from being seriously injured, or worse.

What we did took patience and time, but most of all, it took a lot of love. Seeing Harry still in one piece is our ultimate reward. I firmly believe that if you take a cat into your life, just like a human, you must accept every part of it, the good and the bad, and in Harry's case, the wild.

—*Joyce Stark*

Miracles in Fur Coats

I am not a religious person in the conventional sense. Nor have I been a particularly spiritual one. Yet, I realize that when you most need them, miracles do happen. Furthermore, they come in the form that means the most to you. In my case, on little cat's feet.

It began twenty years ago when a coworker brought me a five-week-old kitten she had rescued. Although I had wanted a kitten to keep Tiger, my one-year-old cat, company, I hadn't envisioned a scrawny, flea-covered bag of bones. Against my better judgment, I took her home. Several flea baths later, she appeared marginally more presentable.

While I had my doubts about her, Sammy quickly decided I made an acceptable mother and attached herself to me. No matter where I went, there she'd be. If I ventured out of her sight, she'd cry. Only cuddling her in my arms calmed her down.

I was holding her the day my mom called to tell me Grandfather had died. He was the only grandfather I had known, and as a child, I had secretly believed I was his favorite. For days after the funeral, I would burst into tears whenever anyone spoke to me. I wanted to lose myself in sleep, but I had a kitten who demanded attention. As I comforted her, I began to be comforted myself. As I told her everything would be all right, I started to believe it. As I told her how much I loved her, I realized I was also loved. My grandfather's death didn't erase his love. As long as I had his memories, he was with me.

Sammy remained my constant companion for sixteen years. Although I still had Tiger and had added a third cat, Thomas, to the household, Sammy held first place in my heart—maybe because she was linked to my grandfather or because she needed me so much. Heartbroken, I vowed never to get another cat. Tiger and Thomas would be enough now.

Two weeks later, on a run to the pet store for food, a bundle of fur caught my eye. Within minutes, a small, tortoiseshell tabby kitten nestled in my arms but I reminded myself I didn't want or need a kitty. Before I could hand her back a sick cat in a nearby cage distracted the clerk. She whisked the cat out of the room, leaving me alone with the wriggling fur ball in my arms. For the next twenty minutes, the kitten stared into my eyes, grabbed my hair, and did everything except shout, *Take me home, we need each other.* I refused to listen. When the clerk returned, she tickled the kitten under the chin, saying, "Isn't she a cutie? She just arrived. Lucky you, you're the first person to hold her, and she obviously likes you. How do you want to pay?"

Pay? I didn't want to pay. I wasn't going to pay.

The next thing I knew, I had a receipt in one hand and a kitten in the other.

Over the next few weeks, Miss Maggie made a place for herself in my home and in my heart. She didn't replace Sammy. Animals, like people, can't be replaced that easily. However, she showed me that even a broken heart has enough love in it to reach out to a kitten in need of love. By reaching out, a broken heart begins to heal itself—a lesson I'd learned once from Sammy but had forgotten.

Looking over the adoption papers, I realized Miss Maggie had been brought to the Humane Society on July 1, Sammy's birthday. Yet she hadn't been put up for adoption for six weeks, although the normal time period is much shorter. The delay in putting Miss Maggie up for adoption, my showing up at the pet store two hours after she had been brought in, and the persistent clerk all added up to one thing: Miss Maggie and I were meant for each other.

It's happening again. Two weeks ago a male kitten wandered into the parking lot of a school where I substitute teach. The principal kept him in her office, but he needed a real home. She asked me to take him, but I refused, because I already had three cats.

But a little voice inside said, *He's going to be yours*. The next morning, I found out why.

Tiger had suffered the feline equivalent of a stroke and lost almost all control of her right side. She could barely walk, eat, or drink and was getting progressively weaker. I knew what I had to do. The next day, with red and swollen eyes, I took her to the vet for the last time.

In a few days, a small black-and-white kitten named Jonesy will come home from school with me. Not to take Tiger's place, but to carve out his own place just as Sammy, Miss Maggie, and Thomas had done before—to show me that life and love go on even in the midst of heartbreak and death.

Miracles do happen. All you have to do is open your eyes, your heart, and your door to them.

—Harriet Cooper

Miss Ellie and Her Babies

"Come on in, darlin'. The door's unlocked," said Miss Ellie.

I was on a scheduled medical visit to check on the elderly woman. Miss Ellie, eighty-five years old, lived alone in a small, one-bedroom house with her two cats, Bogie and Bacall.

As I entered the small living room, a blast of hot dry air from the black wood-burning stove hit me. Miss Ellie was sitting in her worn, green-plaid recliner, practically on top of the hot stove. The petite woman, dressed in a blue flower-print cotton dress and two frayed dark green wool sweaters to keep her warm, smiled brightly as I entered her home. Her full head of snow-white hair looked like it had gotten away from her and caught up in a wind tunnel. Even though her legs were elevated, I could readily see they were edematous.

"How are you feeling, Miss Ellie?" I asked as I checked her blood pressure, which was dangerously high at 190/100.

"Oh, I'm doin' just fine. It's just me and my babies, ya know," she said. "Winter's upon us, though, so I keep myself warm in front of my stove. Been sitting up all night, 'cause it just seems to get colder and colder."

"Miss Ellie, I see your legs are swollen. I need to take off your hose so I can see how puffy they are," I informed her.

"All right, you just do what you need to," she said.

When I tried to remove the dark brown hose from her legs, I was shocked to find they were stuck to her skin like paper on glue. I knew from the dried drainage stains on the stockings and the foul odor coming from the area that her legs were badly infected. I gently started to remove the stockings, but stopped abruptly when I saw that the skin was peeling away with the nylons. I realized then that Miss Ellie had suffered at least second-degree burns on her legs and feet from sitting too close to the stove. With a history of poor circulation, she had little feeling in either leg and hadn't felt the heat from the stove burning her tissues. I knew she needed to be hospitalized immediately to treat the burns, infection, and high blood pressure if she were to survive the winter.

"Miss Ellie, I've got to get you to the hospital today. Your blood pressure is way up, and I think you have infected burns on your legs."

"Oh no, I can't do that!" she cried. "Who will take care of my babies? They're all I have in this world. I'd die without them. Please, please help me." Tears streamed down her sallow cheeks.

The two cats sitting on the arm of Miss Ellie's chair stared at me intently with their green eyes. Bogie was solid black, and his female counterpart, Bacall, was rust colored.

I pondered a solution for the unusual situation I was confronted with. Torn between honoring her wishes and leaving the cats at home to be dealt with later, I followed my conscious.

"Tell you what I can do," I said. "I'll call the ambulance, and we'll take the kitties with us. After I get you settled into the hospital, I'll contact a vet who can board them until you are well enough to come home."

Miss Ellie burst into sobs of relief.

While we waited for the ambulance to arrive, I emptied the contents from my black leather nurse's bag and stuffed the wailing cats inside. That quieted Miss Ellie's tears, but not the screeching cats now zipped into my bag.

The ambulance arrived shortly, and as we loaded Miss Ellie into the back, she held out her thin arms and called out, "My babies, my babies."

"I've got them, Miss Ellie, they're coming with us," I assured her.

I slid into the back of the ambulance with my hidden cargo. The medics didn't see the cats, but I'm sure they wondered what was making all the ruckus inside my nurse's bag. The ambulance left Miss Ellie's home with the lights blinking and the siren wailing. The cats must have thought they were on their way to kitty heaven, because their shrieks soon matched the screaming siren. To calm my patient and my own jangled nerves, I unzipped the bag, and out jumped the cats. They immediately took refuge on Miss Ellie's chest, where they purred contently.

That is the scene that greeted the surprised paramedics when they opened the back door of the ambulance to unload Miss Ellie and wheel her into the hospital. "Don't ask," I said calmly. The wide-eyed looks on the paramedic's faces were nothing compared to the shocked expressions on the physicians' and nurses' faces in the emergency room. I moved along with the stretcher, holding onto the cats to keep them from jumping ship, as they wheeled Miss Ellie into the trauma room. The attending doctor looked at me as though I would make a good candidate for the loony bin. I smiled. "Family," I said nodding to the two felines, whose claws were now imbedded in my blue sweater.

Miss Ellie was admitted for treatment. The cats were boarded for free by a kind local vet.

Miss Ellie had a difficult time adjusting to the hospital and to being separated from her babies. She had suffered second-degree burns over 75 percent of her legs and feet, which required massive amounts of antibiotics, meticulous care of the burned areas, and frequent physical therapy to get her limbs functional again. It was a slow and difficult healing process, and she wasn't responding as well as she should have. To make matters worse, she refused to eat and rested fitfully.

I realized that Miss Ellie was ailing not only from physical trauma but also from emotional distress. She was grieving for her babies. So I made a proposal to her. "If you'll eat and do your exercises, I'll bring your babies in for a visit." She readily agreed to the deal.

How I would accomplish that task, I had no idea. I figured I could conceal the cats in my black leather nurse's bag again, but I hadn't thought about how I would make my way through the hospital corridors without the squirming, squealing stowaways being detected. Yet, somehow, I managed to sneak the cats into the hospital for a few visits. The tricky part was the elevator ride to and from her private room. As expected, the cats would become quite vocal. When they started meowing loudly, I'd feign a deep, open-mouthed yawn, in hopes the people on the elevator would think the noise was coming from me. I didn't have a convincing meow.

Miss Ellie's special hospital visitors had exactly the effect I'd hoped for. Her spirits lifted, she started eating and doing her physical therapy, and her body began to heal. When her burns healed and her blood pressure stabilized, she was allowed to return home with her small creatures. I had a safety cage built around the stove so she couldn't get close enough to cause additional burns. I continued to visit her and monitor her progress, and she continued to live happily with her babies for several years.

The kitty's visits with their mama supported my belief that sometimes it takes more than medicine to heal the body and soul.

—Kay Cavanaugh

The Blessings in Ah-choo!

Generally speaking, folks line up in either one camp or the other. They have certain, definite preferences when it comes to pets. Usually, they are either in the dog-lovers camp or the cat-lovers camp.

Through the years, as my husband and I raised four children, we gave them the opportunity to experience the responsibility of helping care for our pets. While the kids were young, the pets were more ours than theirs—that is, until our son, Patrick, and his sister, Sara, determined to get their own dog. They had in mind a dachshund puppy, but it would cost them $50. So they went to work. The two of them washed cars, sold lemonade, babysat, and did various odd jobs to come up with the money. That feisty little dog followed them around and was their companion and then ours for nineteen years.

But this is not a story about dogs; this is really a tale about cats. We never had a cat as a pet while Sara and Patrick were growing up. Later, I acquired a wonderful Maine coon cat we called Smudge. I say "acquired" because that is how you get a cat. It's generally not intentional; they just kind of show up, and you adopt or you don't. Once I got to know Smudge, there was no question that I wanted him to stay. He seemed to have some of the easygoing character of our black lab, Coal. They became fond companions, often sleeping curled up together on Coal's comfy, old bed.

By then, Patrick and Sara both lived in other places, occasionally coming home for special holidays to see their two younger brothers and us. Sara had developed some allergies, and right at the top of her list was cats, so she avoided the cats when she was in our home. Once, when she was sleeping in an upstairs room, she heard what she described as a loud growling noise. Smudge was coming by to see her. He always purred very loudly. Sara was put off by the noise. After that, in deference to her and her husband's allergies, I kept our two cats in the garage during their visits. Later, two of her four children also showed tendencies to sneeze when around cats, and one, Daniel, developed asthma-like symptoms.

So, although I enjoyed a longtime friendship of twenty years with Smudge—otherwise known as "the king of my heart"—he was never a companion to our daughter's family. In fact, she often referenced cats in a negative way, talking about how she had seen them kill birds or, while living in Omaha, how cats would come by and use their children's sandbox as a litter box—annoying creatures that they were.

In the year that my husband and I packed up and moved from Colorado to Texas, to live closer to a son and his family and to our daughter and her family, we experienced some sad losses. Our cat Samantha, who had been with us fifteen years, developed a mass between her shoulder blades, which turned out to be cancer in the form of a rapidly growing sarcoma. I had to make the tough decision to have her euthanized. Like many cats, Sam had been pretty much of a one-person companion and never really warmed to others in the family, nor they to her.

Several months later, when Smudge began to slow down, withdraw, and eventually stop eating, we were very concerned. He had been a wonderful companion since our lab, Coal, had passed away. I rushed Smudge to a weekend clinic, only to learn, several hundred dollars later, that he had cancer of the liver. We lost this faithful old friend just before Thanksgiving. My kids all knew that I really missed this amazing cat.

Meanwhile, down near Houston where our daughter lives, on Thanksgiving her family heard some faint little "mew" sounds coming from the other side of a high fence that surrounds their backyard. The neighbors, whose yard the sounds were coming from, were out of town. When the sounds persisted, our grandchildren's curiosity got the best of them, and they discovered that a feral cat had delivered a litter of kittens under an old pile of wood that was next to the fence.

Later that week there was a heavy downpour. When Sara and the kids ventured out to check on the kittens, they saw momma cat depositing them one by one out in the front driveway in the rain. There had been six kittens, but one drowned in that old woodpile. Sara and the kids moved the other five kitties into a shed on the neighbor's property. The shed had space under the door so momma cat could come and go. But momma cat moved them again, to another yard where a big dog lived. Sara and the kids found and rescued them after looking high and low. This time they took matters into their own hands and decided to take care of them themselves. They placed the kittens, two black ones and three gray tabbies, in a box in their garage. They bought baby formula and began feeding the kittens.

Sara went online and learned that it is important to handle feral cats while they are young in order to train them to be friendly, to domesticate them. So the children handled them, even bringing them into the house, much to the chagrin of their two dogs. One black kitten had white paws and a white bib, so they named her Tuxedo, and the other they called Panther. Since the kittens would be ready to go to new homes just after Christmas, they gave two of them Christmas names, Mistletoe and Holly. Our grandson Daniel's favorite Winnie the Pooh character is Tigger, so that name was given to the only male in the litter, a short-haired, striped tabby.

Just after Christmas Sara and John and the kids drove up to Austin to spend the weekend with us. I heard the car arrive in the drive followed by doors slamming and excited laughter as the kids tumbled through the open door and deposited two darling kittens into my arms. "Merry Christmas, Nana!" they shouted.

Even more heartwarming to me than the gift of two new cats to keep us company was the change I saw in our daughter's family. They had laid aside their previous disdain for cats and risked allergic reactions to rescue and take care of these kittens. They placed all in welcoming homes, especially blessing us! Incidentally, our last name is Wood, so we have Tigger Wood and Holly Wood. Both are delightful, full of all the antics and curiosity that are endearing about cats, and as celebrated as their namesakes.

—Mahala E. Wood

Contributors

Monica A. Andermann ("Cat's Choice") lives on Long Island with her husband, Bill, and their cat, Charley. She is currently working toward a bachelor of fine arts in creative writing, realizing a lifelong dream of becoming a writer. She urges all readers to follow their dreams and to support their local animal shelters.

Murr Brewster ("Larry: Not Much of a Cat, but Oh, What a Gal!") will retire soon after thirty-one years as a letter carrier in Portland, Oregon. She enjoys hiking, gardening, playing piano, doing artwork, and writing, and hopes to do much more of it in the company of a new kitty, as yet unplucked.

Marcia E. Brown ("A Cat Named Bob" and "Mr. Momma Cat") is an Austin, Texas, freelance writer specializing in humor and enjoys preserving stories from her childhood for her family. Her tales have been widely published in magazines, newspapers, and anthologies, and several have won awards. This is her fourth publication in the *Cup of Comfort* book series.

Ada Nicholson Brownell ("One Creature Great and Small") is a freelance writer living in Springfield, Missouri. Her writing currently appears in *A Cup of Comfort for Christians*, *What I Learned from God While Cooking*, and *50 Tough Questions*.

Linda Bruno ("Raggedy Andy") of Ocala, Florida, is a speaker and writer. She is writing a devotional book based on how our interactions with pets mirror our relationship with God. She and her husband, Guy, have two cats, one dog, a grown daughter, five grandchildren, and several grandpets.

Leslie Ann Budewitz ("Hail to the Queen") is a writer and lawyer in Bigfork, Montana, at the foot of the Swan Mountains, where she bravely fends off the snowshoe hares and whitetail deer intent on nipping the flowers that grow on Autumn's grave.

Amanda Callendrier ("Nobody Gets Left Behind") lives in France, where she is a full-time mommy to Justine and David and to Margot the cat. In her spare time, she writes short stories and generally keeps the litter box clean.

Jean Campion ("Smoky's Journey") is a "free-range" writer, editor, and tutor. A retired teacher, she works from her country home in southwest Colorado. *Minta Forever*, her historical novel, grew out of a research project she did on one-room schools. She is married and the mother of three. One cat currently deigns to reside with her.

Kay Cavanaugh ("Miss Ellie and Her Babies") is a retired nurse educator living in Powder Springs, Georgia. She does volunteer work with a local senior center, teaches health-related classes, takes adult education classes, and keeps fit by practicing yoga and water aerobics.

Loy Michael Cerf ("Ozzie to the Rescue"), an animal-loving, Chicago-area freelance writer, enjoys making blankets for Project Linus and dreaming up creative ways to coerce her grown children into pet-sitting so that said author can guiltlessly cruise the globe with her husband of thirty-something years.

Keri Ann Collins ("Fraidy Cat") lives in Kasilof, Alaska, where she is currently a married, stay-at-home mom with seven terrific kids. When she's not running her children around everywhere, she likes to snowmobile, to ride four-wheelers, and to build log furniture. She has a bachelor of arts in creative writing from Linfield College.

Harriet Cooper ("Miracles in Fur Coats") is a freelance writer who lives in Toronto, Canada, with her three cats. Her humor, essays, articles, short stories, and poetry have appeared in newspapers, magazines, Web sites, newsletters, anthologies, radio, and a coffee can. She specializes in writing about family, relationships, cats, psychology, and health.

J. M. Cornwell ("Phantom of the Apartment") lives in the Colorado Rockies, where she divides her time between writing and work. She has no pets, but keeps her closets available for visiting friends and their pets. She has been published in *Chicken Soup* and *Haunted Encounters*. Her novel, *Past Imperfect*, debuted in January 2008.

Sheila Crosby ("The Whole Kitten Caboodle") lives in the Spanish Canary Islands. She originally moved there from the United Kingdom to work at an astronomical observatory and stayed on after she was "downsized." Her hobbies include cooking, laundry, ironing, and cleaning the house. Unfortunately, she's so busy writing a thriller set in the observatory that she rarely gets a chance for hobbies.

Mary Margret Daughtridge ("Crystal Blue Persuasion") lives with Crystal the Cat in North Carolina. She's an artist, spiritual coach, metaphysician, and teacher. As if that weren't enough, her friend Diane demanded she add "writer" to that list. Her first novel, *SEALed with a Kiss*, debuts from Sourcebooks in 2008. Diane made her do it.

Maria Dean ("A Cat in the Bag") lives in Bradford, England, with her husband, Ryan, and their three cats, Dylan, Hendrix, and Layla. She works at her local school as a learning mentor while studying for a degree in creative writing. Currently working on a series of short stories, Maria hopes to fulfill her ambition to become a full-time writer.

Jennifer DiCamillo ("Creepy Cat") is an award-winning writer and a motivational speaker. She is the author of *The Price of Peace, Courting Disaster, Deadknots, Despicado, Passing Thoughts,* and *Passing Images.* Her work has also been published in the *Big Boys* children's book series, *Unbelievable Stories* magazine, *A Cup of Comfort for Women in Love, Ozarks* magazine, and *Amazon Shorts.*

Miralee Ferrell ("Mountain Mama and the Man of Her Heart") lives in the Pacific Northwest, has been married thirty-five years, has two grown children, and is active in her church. Writing is a passion, and her first novel was released in October 2007. She and her husband are looking forward to cruising on their fifty-one-foot sailboat next summer, where creative writing opportunities will abound.

Elizabeth King Gerlach ("Cat Prints on the Volvo") is a writer living in Eugene, Oregon. She's authored two books on autism and is currently working on children's books.

Denise R. Graham ("One of a Kind") is the author of two young reader fantasy/mysteries, *Eye of Fortune* and *Curse of the Lost Grove*. Her stories have appeared in *A Cup of Comfort for Writers*, two *Magic the Gathering* anthologies, and *Woman's World*. She lives near St. Louis, Missouri, with her husband, the inimitable Ron Morris. She's a Writers Under the Arch groupie.

Dena Harris ("Dibbs!" and "Why My Cat May Someday Cost Me My Marriage") is an award-winning writer and speaker. Her humor collection, *Lessons In Stalking: Adjusting to Life With Cats*, is available in bookstores and online. She lives in Madison, North Carolina, with her husband and two cats.

Wayne Hill ("Calico Bob and the Bamboo Viper") left Montana to travel the world with the U.S. Navy and as a commercial pilot. His cats of various shapes and sizes accompanied him throughout his adventures. He currently lives in the Dallas area with his wife, Roslyn, and their cats, Audrey, Rebecca, and Belle Starr.

Ann Newton Holmes ("The Purrfect Cure") resides with her husband on a hillside overlooking the Napa Valley in a house they designed and built with their own hands. Retired from education, she has coauthored two coffee-table books on Hindu architecture and mythology. But fiction remains her passion. She has written two novels set in Rajasthan and many short stories rooted in India as well as in a childhood spent fishing the West with her nomadic parents.

Allison Johnson ("Taming Miss Jazzy"), a novelist and coauthor of a parenting book, lives in Southern California with her husband and teenage daughter. When not involved in cat taming or other dangerous activities, she's behind her desk working on her next project.

Kathleen R. Jorgensen ("Man's Best Friend") lives in Richmond, Virginia, with her husband, Jorgie, and their cat, Ben. She has wanted to write since she first heard fairy tales as a child. When not spending time with her family or running her billing business, Kathleen writes women's fiction and mystery novels.

Lyndell King ("Scratch That") writes romantic comedy and suspense under the pen name Babe King. She lives in Tasmania, Australia, with her husband, two homeschooled boys, and a variety of animals domestic and wild—though none so wild as her boys.

Anne Krist ("Papa and Misha") lives an exciting life with her consultant husband of thirty-four years. They travel around the United States for his work, allowing them the chance to live in a variety of locations and giving Anne a chance to scout out new and interesting settings for her books and stories.

Holly Leigh ("Dream Cat") has published essays and poetry on travel, medical, equine, and nature topics. She was not truly cat-inspired until after college, when a suave tuxedo named Gatsby adopted her. She now lives in Ipswich, Massachusetts, with Vindaloo, an orange shelter cat, and Jaspurr, a Bengal-cross.

Shawn Daywalt Lutz ("Cat People") lives in Capistrano Beach, California, with her husband, two children, and their beloved Diego. A retired actress and singer, Shawn enjoys being with her family, exploring California, and writing. This is her second publication in the *Cup of Comfort* book series.

Allison Maher ("Brotherly Love") lives on a small farm in rural Nova Scotia, Canada, with her husband and two sons. In the off season, she writes young adult novels for Thistledown Press.

Nancy Marano ("The Fleece Robe"), a freelance writer living in Albuquerque, New Mexico, has written articles for many local and national publications. She currently writes for and edits *PETroglyphs*, an award-winning regional animal newspaper, and is working on a children's book. Though she writes on a variety of subjects, her passion is animals.

Elaine Young McGuire ("Max, the 'Stupid' Cat") is a retired teacher residing in Lilburn, Georgia. Since 1995, when she first began submitting her writing, more than 100 of her stories, devotionals, and poems have appeared in a variety of periodicals and anthologies. Her work has also been published in several languages.

Eileen Mitchell ("Confessions of a Naked Cat Lover") is an award-winning writer from suburban Chicago. A 2007 winner of the Thurber Humor Writing Contest and second-place winner of the 2006 Will Rogers Writing Contest sponsored by the National Society of Newspaper Columnists, she also writes a pet column called "Hollywood Tails." Petpals include Montycat, Maggie, and Molly.

Patricia Mitchell ("Say What? The Serious Business of Naming a Cat"), former editorial director with Hallmark Cards, is a freelance writer specializing in Bible studies, inspirational articles, gift books, and Christian devotionals. In her spare time, she fills food bowls, scratches chins, and scoops poop. She and her cats call Kansas City, Missouri, their home.

Gary Presley ("Silky and the Woman Whose Hair Smelled Nice") lives in Springfield, Missouri. He has written for publications as diverse as Salon.com, *Notre Dame* magazine, and *The Ozark Mountaineer*. His memoir will be published in Fall 2008 by the University of Iowa Press.

Gail Pruszkowski ("The Power of the Purr") is a lifelong resident of Philadelphia, Pennsylvania. She works for the Philly Water Department as a drafting supervisor while pursuing her love of reading, writing, and reviewing for *Romantic Times BOOKreviews* magazine. Her two furry collaborators eagerly await the day she will be a stay-at-home writer.

Marcia Rudoff ("My Life as the Other Woman") teaches memoir-writing classes at the Bainbridge Island Senior Center and is a newspaper columnist for the *Bainbridge Review*. Her stories and personal essays have appeared in magazines, newspapers, and anthologies, including the *Cup of Comfort* and *Rocking Chair Reader* series. Her book, *We've Got Stories, Where Are Yours?* is a guide for writing a memoir. Her other interests include her children, grandchildren, baseball, and chocolate.

Diana Schmitt ("Ranch Kitties") lives on a ranch in southwest Colorado with her husband, Jerry. Together, they run several hundred head of cattle in Colorado and New Mexico. She is also a registered nurse and certified legal nurse consultant. Her hobbies include writing, gardening, and canning.

Susan M. Schulz ("Wild Thing, You Moved Me") is a Bible teacher, writer, wife, and mother of three who lives in Woodstock, Georgia, during the week but on her farm on the weekends. Her passion to encourage God's children to hear his magnificent voice has birthed Listening Heart Ministry.

Julie F. Smith ("True Love") lives with her teenaged daughters Stephanie and Madeline in the Crowsnest Pass in southwestern Alberta, Canada. She works as an administrative assistant and has been writing since she learned to read.

Connie Spittler ("A Universal Language"), of Tucson, Arizona, is known for her workshops on Georgia O'Keeffe and on journaling. Her four-volume *Wise Women* DVD series was selected for Harvard University's Schlesinger Library on the History of Women in America. Her award-winning essays, short stories, and poetry appear in anthologies, journals, and magazines.

Joyce Stark ("Gangsta Tabby") lives in Northeast Scotland and has recently retired from local government. She has written a book about her many travels throughout the United States and recently completed her second book on teaching a second language to younger children.

Kim H. Striker ("A Star-Crossed Romance") is a freelance writer living and working on a farm in the Crown of Maine with her husband and three cats, Starlight, Smokey Bear, and Hutch. Her publishing credits include short stories in national romance magazines and nonfiction pieces in anthologies and professional journals.

Judy Swanson ("The Only Good Cat Dad Ever Met") lives in Spring Lake, Michigan, with her husband, Alan, and her cat, Prinz. Recently retired from a career in human resources management, she uses her newfound free time to enjoy and write about grandchildren, golf, bicycling, beach walking, travel, family, friends, and, of course, the cat.

Sarah Wagner ("A Purrfect Match") is a writer living in West Virginia with her husband, sons, and a small zoo. You can find her work in *Red River Review, The Harrow's Midnight Lullabies,* and *Gryphonwood.*

Pat Wahler ("Motherly Ties") earned a master's degree in nonprofit management and served as a board member for the St. Charles Humane Society. Her writing has received recognition in the areas of poetry and fiction. She resides with her husband and a schnauzer with attitude in Missouri, where they are rediscovering life without children at home.

Mahala E. Wood ("The Blessings in *Ah-choo!*") and her husband, Tom, left Colorado's mountains three years ago to live near their children and eight grandkids. Having enjoyed a twenty-two-year Navy career, she is no stranger to new places. They have resided in Panama, Maryland, California, Oregon, Colorado, and now Texas. She enjoys reading and has recently pursued a desire to write. Her family and pets inspire her writing.

Laurel Yourke ("When the Time Is Right") is the author of *Take Your Characters to Dinner: Creating the Illusion of Reality in Fiction* and *Waiting for Beethoven,* a poetry collection. She resides in Madison, Wisconsin, where she teaches at the University of Wisconsin–Madison in the Department of Liberal Studies and the Arts.

About the Editor

Colleen Sell has compiled and edited more than twenty volumes of the *Cup of Comfort*® book series. A veteran writer and editor, she has authored, ghost-written, or edited more than a hundred books; published scores of magazine articles and essays; and served as editor-in-chief of two award-winning magazines, associate editor of a national business magazine, and home and garden columnist of a regional newsmagazine. She and the love of her midlife, T. N. Trudeau, make their home in the Pacific Northwest in a turn-of-the-century farmhouse, which they are slowly renovating, on forty acres, which they are slowly turning into a blueberry and lavender farm.